INDEXING
The State of Our Knowledge and the State of Our Ignorance

*Proceedings of the 20th Annual Meeting
of the American Society of Indexers
New York City, May 13, 1988*

Edited by Bella Hass Weinberg

Learned Information, Inc.
Medford, NJ
1989

Copyright © 1989 by   Learned Information, Inc.
                       143 Old Marlton Pike
                       Medford, NJ 08055

Printed in the United States of America

Cover Design: Patrick F. Holman

Library of Congress Cataloging-in-Publication Data

American Society of Indexers. Meeting (20th : 1988 :
    New York, N.Y.)
    Indexing : the state of our knowledge and the state
of our ignorance.

    Includes bibliographies and index.
    1. Indexing—Congresses. I. Weinberg, Bella Hass.
II. American Society of Indexers. III. Title.
Z695.9.A52 1988   025.3   89-2452
ISBN 0-938734-32-6

To my mother, Roza Weissman Hass,
a master of organization.
With Love,
Bella

CONTENTS

Preface

The themes of papers presented at Annual Meetings of the American Society of Indexers have tended to be practical—"How to operate an indexing business" or "How to use microcomputer-based indexing software."

The theme of the 20th Annual Meeting—"Indexing: The State of Our Knowledge and The State of Our Ignorance"—is also practical, in the sense of the proverb "There is nothing so practical as a good theory." The papers do not present esoteric theories, but rather a distillation of the key ideas on the art of indexing, which, we hope, can be applied in practice.

Indexing has been renamed by other professional societies. Some of the synonymous terms (euphemisms?) include: *documentation, content analysis*, and *information representation*. Although the job title "information specialist" generally commands a higher salary than that of "indexer," the requisite skills are basically the same. Evidence for the complexity of the indexer's task is found in the fact that artificial intelligence researchers are currently focusing on *categorization* and *summarization* of text—which we call *classification* and *indexing*. Indexers can offer millennia of experience in extracting information from text and organizing it for use, but it seems that it is difficult to reduce the principles to an algorithm that a computer can apply.

The distinguished participants in this conference examine those principles—that is, the state of our knowledge of indexing—and also touch on what we do not know, i.e., the state of our ignorance, and suggest research that needs to be done.

It is hoped that this compilation will be of practical use to indexers as well as stimulating to theorists of information science.

Bella Hass Weinberg
Program Chair

Acknowledgments

Conference planning is in many ways like indexing: it demands a sense of organization, attention to detail, and a compulsion for follow-up and verification. The two activities differ in that an indexer generally works alone, while a conference planner is dependent on the cooperation of many individuals, who often work behind the scenes. These people are generally recognized by a brief mention during the conference or by inclusion of their names in the printed program, which is ephemeral.

The publication of the proceedings of the 20th anniversary meeting of the American Society of Indexers affords me the opportunity to thank those who helped make the conference possible in a volume that I hope will be referred to for many years to come.

First—the speakers, all of whom are prominent experts in their fields. I am grateful to these busy people who honored their commitments to present the commissioned papers and submit them in documented form for publication.

Second—the people who assisted me in putting the Annual Meeting together in my capacity as Vice President of the American Society of Indexers: Bettie Jane Third, ASI Director, who handled registration; Trina E. King, ASI Recording Secretary, in charge of local arrangements; and Harris Shupak, Chair of ASI's Publications Committee, who handled printing and mailing of the conference brochure and program. Mrs. Rhonda Kleiman, my Graduate Assistant in the Division of Library and Information Science at St. John's University, typed much of the voluminous correspondence related to the meeting.

Tom Hogan, organizer of the National Online Meeting—of which ASI's 20th Annual Meeting was a satellite event—was of great help in planning the facilities and catering for the conference at the Sheraton Centre. It has been a pleasure to work with Mr. Hogan on this book as well, in his capacity as President of Learned Information.

Since assuming the Presidency of the American Society of Indexers at the 1988 Annual Meeting, I have been grateful for the support of the staff and faculty of the Division of Library and Information Science at St. John's University, notably its Director, Dr. Emmett Corry. The research leave granted me by the University in the Fall of 1988 afforded me the time to devote to the editing of this volume and directing the complex affairs of ASI.

Finally, I thank my husband, Gerard, and daughter, Kira, for putting up with my crazy schedule and tolerating the mountains of unindexed papers that adorn our home.

B.H.W.

Editor's Note

The first person has been retained in the published papers, but they are not exact transcripts of the oral presentations. Some stylistic editing has been done to enhance readability of the papers.

The presentation of ten state-of-the-art papers in a one-day conference, each preceded by an introduction to the theme and biographical data on the speaker, did not leave much time for comments or questions from the audience. These have therefore not been included in the proceedings, but in a few cases, comments from the audience have been incorporated into the edited papers.

Audiocassettes of the full conference are available from Minute-Tapes International.

B.H.W.

The Literature of Indexing: Introduction to the Theme

In planning the program for this meeting, it seemed to me that if you want to assess the state of our knowledge about indexing, the first thing you would want to know is where the research literature is found. In the general introduction, I alluded to the variation in indexing terminology; this is reflected in the scatter of the indexing literature.

There is a journal called The Indexer, *sponsored by four indexing societies; but as I noted in my review of this journal in* Library and Information Science Annual *(v.3, 1987), it is not the first periodical to which an indexing researcher is likely to submit a paper. When I thought about who could best survey the literature of indexing, it was obvious that it had to be Dr. Hans Wellisch, who has compiled two book-length bibliographies on indexing* (Indexing and Abstracting: An International Bibliography. *Clio Press, 1980; 1984) and supplements them through a current awareness bibliography in* The Indexer. *Whenever I publish a paper on indexing, I always send Hans a reprint and worry that he will tell me that it is completely unoriginal and redundant with the prior literature; therefore, when I invited him to give this paper, I was particularly pleased to learn that the proposed topic had never been treated in the literature before.*

Dr. Hans H. Wellisch came to the United States from Israel, where he had been the head of a technical information center. He is now Professor Emeritus at the College of Library and Information Services at the University of Maryland, where he received his Ph.D. in 1975. Professor Wellisch's interests center on all aspects of bibliographic control, with special emphasis on subject indexing as well as on linguistic aspects of information science, the physical planning of libraries, and the history of library and information work. He is active in the International Federation for Documentation (FID) as a contributor to the Universal Decimal Classification and its development. He is a member and former President of the American Society of Indexers, which he represents on the American National Standard Institute's Committee Z39 (Library and Information Science), now called the National Information Standards Organization. He is also a member of several other professional societies and associations, and was a founder and former secretary of the Israel Society of Special Libraries and Information Centers. Professor Wellisch received the first H. W. Wilson Award for

1

Excellence in Indexing for the index he compiled for his own book, The Conversion of Scripts *(Wiley, 1978). He has published a number of books and many articles and reports on all aspects of his professional interests.*

B.H.W.

The Literature of Indexing

Hans H. Wellisch

What people think, say, or do about *indexes* and *indexing*—interpreting these concepts in their widest possible sense as denoting any device that helps to find and pinpoint stored and recorded information, and the construction of such devices respectively—is reflected in the professional literature, the repository of both our knowledge of these topics and of our ignorance—the latter, as I shall argue, in more than one way.

The Past Seven Years

Surveying the indexing literature of the past seven years is not as easily done as in the two previous published summaries of "vital statistics" of abstracting and indexing (A&I) (Wellisch, 1980; 1985), which were based on comprehensive and multilingual bibliographies, comprising material up to 1981. The items listed in my current-awareness bibliography published in *The Indexer* have to be chosen according to much more stringent criteria, owing to the limited space available, and also because of certain self-imposed limitations (mainly concerning the elimination of items in lesser-known languages for which there is probably little if any interest on the part of the members of the several indexing societies that sponsor the journal). To make such choices, I am still trying to cover as much as possible of the A&I literature by scanning many dozens of journals and culling items from the major abstracting services in print and online, which gives me a fairly good overview of the scene, and allows me to make some generalizations (not all of which may be to your liking).

The A&I literature still seems to obey Bradford's Law of Scattering,[1] though its core of high-yield journals, in which most of the relevant articles are published, is somewhat larger than that of other fields, and the "tail" of one-shot contributions on indexing in unlikely or out-of-the-way journals is rather long (though, for the reasons just cited, I cannot produce numerical data).

I tend to think that the wide scattering of writings on indexing is an indication of the fact that the making of indexes is still not widely recognized as a professional task, and perhaps not even as a craft that has to be learned by doing, following rules of good practice which have evolved over a long time, and which are truly mastered by only relatively few indexers.

Indeed, as we all know, to our regret, indexing is often believed to be so simple that anyone armed with a rudimentary knowledge of the ABC and a yellow highlighting pen can easily do it, not to mention PC (personal computer) programs able to pick out words not on a stop list from any text, and sort them automatically (if not quite always intelligibly), thus producing the perfect index. Consequently, everybody and his uncle (or aunt) feels free to rush into print with good advice on how to produce such a perfect index, and unscrupulous editors starved for manuscripts publish the stuff.

A case in point is the computer programmer who reduced all indexing to five simple rules, and proudly published his unfailing recipe in the journal *Byte* (Pountain, 1987).[2]

But even serious and valuable contributions to the literature of indexing do not always appear in the best-known journals of information science and library work, and it is necessary to scan a large number of rather divergent professional journals, as well as the A&I services specifically covering the fields of information and library science if one wishes to keep tabs on what is currently being published.

Indexing and Abstracting Services

Almost by definition, the A&I services or databases dealing with the literature of information work ought to be shining examples of what a first-class service of this type should be. Unfortunately, practically all of them fall more or less short of being good, or even acceptable, examples.

The American *Information Science Abstracts* (ISA) espouses the view that indexing and descriptive cataloging are one and the same thing, lumping together items on both topics indiscriminately in a single section, which shows a remarkable lack of understanding of fundamentals on the part of the editors. *ISA* is prone to outrageous misspellings of authors' names which, once made in the bibliographic listing, are of course automatically replicated in the monthly and annual indexes, which also suffer from the unfortunately widespread syndrome of "initials only" for given names, thus making the identification of Browns, Johnsons, Millers and Smiths impossible in some cases. Not infrequently, articles are listed under the incorrect title of a journal, thus ensuring that the item can never be found and retrieved. Foreign titles are sometimes translated, but are often given only in an English paraphrase, without any indication that this is not the original title—a pernicious practice that also makes effective retrieval difficult, if not impossible.

The other American database from which items on A&I may be culled is the H. W. Wilson Company's *Library Literature*. On the positive side, its coverage is fairly broad and international (though American sources predominate), and its time lag is short—sometimes as little as a few weeks for English-language sources, and quite reasonable for foreign sources in the printed version; it is now also available online on *Wilsonline*, which is even faster, as well as on CD-ROM (compact disc–read only memory) with quarterly updates. All foreign titles are cited in the original or in Romanized form, followed by an English translation in brackets. The database is, however, strictly an indexing service, and does not provide abstracts. A sort of micro-annotation or mini-abstract is sometimes provided for uninformative titles through the addition of a few explanatory words in brackets following the title, but this is no substitute for abstracts, the provision of which should be a future goal of the database's producers.

The British *Library and Information Science Abstracts (LISA)*, though providing very broad international coverage of journals, has time lags of up to two years, even for English-language sources, and more for foreign-language publications. Like its American counterpart, *LISA* is also marred by an intolerably high number of misprints affecting authors' names and titles (especially foreign ones) as well as abstracts, all of which remain uncorrected when the print version is electronically enshrined on CD-ROM silver platters.

The Soviet *Information Abstracts*, produced in Moscow in what the local editors and abstractors think is English, of course offers excellent coverage of Soviet and East Bloc publications, as well as Japanese literature, but its time lag is also considerable, owing to the fact that the service is a translation of the Russian original *Informatika*, one of the many sections of *Referativnyi Zhurnal*, published by VINITI, the central Soviet agency dealing with scientific and technical information. The fact that this service is reaching the U.S. only with great delay (the October 1987 issue arrived here in April 1988), and is available in only very few libraries practically rules it out as a viable source of current information on indexing.

The French *PASCAL THEMA. (Section) T 205 Sciences de l'information. Documentation* (formerly *Bulletin signalétique* 101) has good coverage, including Soviet, East European, and Japanese sources, and, as would be expected, French ones not covered by any other service. Its time lag is often only a few months, but its abstracts are very brief and sometimes nonexistent;

moreover, they are in French, which is read by few Americans. Its subject indexes are, however, also presented in English. Like its Soviet counterpart, this A&I service is available in the U.S. in only a small number of libraries, yet it deserves to be known and used more widely.

The Languages of Indexing Literature

Indexing literature is being published in quite a number of languages, although given the limitations on the current-awareness bibliography mentioned above, it is not possible to provide numerical data to compare with those offered in my previous surveys. As before, however, there can be no doubt that English is the predominant language of publication, employed not only by its native speakers, but also by an increasing number of authors whose mother tongue is a different one (myself included), followed in descending order by Russian, German, French, Japanese, Chinese, Spanish, Slavic languages other than Russian, Scandinavian languages, Hungarian, Finnish, and several other tongues. Most of the authors of contributions in the "tail-end" languages do not offer anything new, but are just trying to bring to the attention of their compatriot indexers and librarians issues that have already been widely discussed in the literature of the major languages. At the same time, these authors deal with knotty problems that are specific to indexing in their particular language. (This evaluation is based on the perusal of English and French-language abstracts rather than on the primary literature in "minor" languages, most of which I am not able to read.)

Regarding the major languages, the approach to certain issues, particularly automatic methods, seems to be markedly different according to language group. English-language literature (most of it American) tends to focus on methods that rely on word or word-stem matching and proximity as well as frequency measures, while paying relatively little or no attention to underlying linguistic problems. German and Russian authors, on the other hand, seem to stress the linguistic approach, possibly because inflected languages offer more possibilities for the automatic recognition of semantic and syntactic features on which all indexing ultimately depends. A little-known, yet remarkable aspect of Soviet research into indexing languages is the attempt to design algorithms that can cope with English text and with linguistic features of the English language, especially for the purpose of automatic abstracting of patents (e.g., Polonskaya, 1986—one of many similar articles). I am not aware of any equivalent or parallel indexing-oriented research on Russian text undertaken in an English-speaking country.

Themes and Rhemes

What are our literature's *themes*, the topics already well-known and often discussed, both in the past and now; and what are its *rhemes*, the new and singular aspects of the themes? Among the former are the perennial accounts of "How I (or, more often nowadays, 'we') indexed such-and-such," to which is almost inevitably added "on our new ABC microcomputer, using XYZ indexing software." These mostly rather boring accounts of every-day professional practice may do wonders for their authors' egos and, as I indicated above, they are published by editors hungry for manuscripts, but they do not, for the most part, really enrich indexing literature, and perhaps a moratorium on such contributions should be called.

Then we have those who only recently joined the ranks of indexers, and discovered to their great astonishment that there are problems with, for example, the sorting of numerals and symbols, the inclusion or exclusion of prepositions when alphabetizing sub-entries, or the question of where to put "see also" references and the like—all of which have by now been dealt with in national and international standards and rules, except that novices (and many oldtimers, too) are ignorant of these, and thus feel compelled to invent their own rules and publish them for what they think will be of benefit to other indexers. Editors should wield the blue pencil or the erase button more often and more heavily.

Lest you think that I am only finding fault with the present state of the literature of indexing, let me state emphatically that I believe that some of the best work in information science has been produced in just those publications that deal with the realm of indexing. These are indeed the ones that can claim to make the information field scientific, not only in name, but in fact. For the past three decades, some of the best minds in this field have at one time or another been engaged in truly scientific research on the fundamentals of indexing, including its relationships with linguistics, psychology, statistics and other branches of mathematics, epistemology, and history, all of which has had a decisive influence on the quality, scope, and effectiveness of indexing.

As to the rhemes of our literature (deliberately stretching the meaning of this concept to fit my present purpose), I seem to discern them in the recent writings of some of the most profound and prolific writers on information science, and indexing in particular. I am referring to two papers that appeared in a series commissioned by the editor of the *Journal of the American Society for Information Science* to reflect on the past three decades of information work. The articles by Salton (1987) and Swanson (1988) (I refer to the latter in more detail below), summing up their experiences, culminate in hitherto all-too-rare insights into the limits of automation in information retrieval, which sets these papers apart from almost all other current discourse on that topic.

Automatic Indexing

The favorite topic these days is, of course, *automatic indexing* or, for short, AI_1 (the subscript "one" being necessary to distinguish it from AI_2, which stands for *artificial intelligence*, the latter often being employed to generate the former). I have labelled it "one" because it is by far the older of the two AIs, people having busied themselves with it for thirty years or so. When Hans Peter Luhn first published his method of automatic indexing (Luhn, 1959), it was new, it was unique, it was exciting; it was, if you wish, a rheme in the discourse on indexing—and it worked. *Keyword-in-Context*, or KWIC indexing, is still the only fully automatic indexing method that works, except, of course, that it is neither quick (for the user), nor is it indexing in the sense of concept indication independent of the vagaries of verbal expression. Since then, a large number of papers, reports, and books have been written on AI_1; many different and ingenious methods have been proposed; and sizable amounts of the taxpayers' money have been spent on research in the field; yet the results are not readily discernible to the naked eye outside of strictly controlled laboratory situations.

The relationship between publications on AI_1 and practical applications in the real world can best be expressed by one of the mathematical formulae so beloved by writers on the topic, to wit:

$$N_{AI} = \frac{1}{AP^2}\ K$$

where N_{AI} is the number of practical applications, A is the number of authors, P is the number of publications on AI_1, and K is a constant yet to be established by a team of Chinese and Korean statisticians at Cornell University.

Regarding AI_2 (artificial intelligence) and its applications to AI_1 (automatic indexing), the literature is also quite voluminous, and about equally divided among English, German and Russian contributions. As in practically all attempts to harness AI_2 to truly intellectual tasks (as distinct from industrial robot work or computer-assisted image enhancing and interpretation), the purportedly successful applications take place in extremely limited "domains" or for closely circumscribed subjects in the (not always articulated) hope that the methods used can be extrapolated and upscaled to cope with real-world problems in information retrieval. So much for what is currently being done in order to advance and expand our knowledge of indexing.

The Ignorance of Indexing

As to the ignorance, it is, as I stated in the beginning, of two kinds. The first is the ignorance of people about what other workers in the field have already said (often much better and with less technical jargon). This is a fault that writers on indexing share with many other professionals who are no longer conversant with their own literature—past as well as present—and it is, of course, largely caused by the ever-increasing information overload with which we are all faced. This kind of ignorance could be reduced (though it can never be eliminated) by editors and review boards, who ought to reject writings that should never see the light of day because of low quality of research, bad writing, or simply because they are merely rehashes of old stuff.

While this kind of ignorance is merely tedious and boring, another kind is more serious, and even dangerous. It manifests itself in the bright-eyed and bushy-tailed expositions of a brave new world in which all or most questions will be dealt with by machines, which will also execute the subsequent search and retrieval of information unfailingly and to the full satisfaction of the inquirer. The authors of such utopian prognostications seem to be woefully ignorant of the mounting evidence on the limits to totally automatic information retrieval (including indexing as its most crucial element). They would be well advised to take note of the studies done during the past decade or so—particularly the one by our incoming president (Weinberg, 1981)—that document the inadequacy of purely mechanical methods, including those relying on various statistical parameters. These authors should also study the "postulates of impotence," that is, reasoned statements of what is impossible to do in information retrieval, recently stated in a paper that deserves to become a classic (Swanson, 1988).

No one would deny that machines are already making the task of the indexer and information-seeker and retriever much easier by taking the drudgery out of the routine work necessary to find the information that people want or need (which, as we now know, is almost never the same, nor is it the same as that which people ask for). Yet those who put their faith in the unfailing power of machines to understand an inquirer's question expressing his or her information want or need—and then find that information—seem to be the victims of a particularly vicious form of reductionism based on the view of the physical world that prevailed until the middle of this century, but which is now seen to be a fallacy. It was based on the belief that the laws of physics (inasmuch as we know them) govern the material world, at least under ideal and sometimes purely theoretical conditions, and that the results of any physical operations, processes, or events are therefore in principle fully predictable.

The latest discoveries have, however, shown that, in the words of the eminent physicist Freeman Dyson, "When we examine matter in finest detail in the experiments of particle physics, we see it behaving as an active agent rather than as an inert substance. Its actions are in the strict sense unpredictable. It makes what appear to be arbitrary choices between alternative possibilities. Between matter as we observe it in the laboratory and mind as we observe it in our own consciousness, there seems to be only a difference in degree but not in kind" (Dyson, 1988, p.8).

Now if something considered as stable and subject to mathematically expressible laws of matter, energy, and time turns out to be essentially unpredictable, how can we ever hope to pin down the infinitely varied expressions of an information want or need, and to match it "automatically" with equally variable and forever changing expressions used by those who want to convey information to others? Listen to Dyson again: "To me, the most astounding fact in the universe . . . is the power of mind which drives my fingers as I write. Somehow, by natural processes still mysterious, [the] brain working . . . in a human skull [has] the power to dream, to calculate, to see and to hear, to speak and to listen, to translate thoughts and feelings into marks on paper which other brains can interpret" (ibid., p.118).

Dyson says "Other *brains*," not machines, because the most basic fact about information (whatever it is) remains irrefutable: it is created by human beings for the use of other human beings. Another basic fact is that the human beings on either end of the information transmission chain are unpredictable, using language as their communication tool, which is also inherently unpredictable and not entirely reducible to rules (*pace* Chomsky) as far as meaning is concerned.

It is ignorance about these fundamental facts that is so blatantly displayed in the writings of those who would convince us that the solution to the problems of information retrieval will be found in the automatic matching of the words of an inquirer with those recorded in retrievable form by other people, whether contemporaries or those of the distant past. Sprucing up this basic contention with the bells and whistles of frequency, probability, and even with (mostly fallacious, if not outright fraudulent) measures of relevance does not make it less of a dangerous illusion. Why dangerous? Because it may become a menace to both indexers and index users. Indexers need not be convinced that picking out words from a text by tagging them and then sorting them alphabetically is not the same as good or even acceptable indexing.

But publishers are apparently enthusiastic about the idea, as are other sectors of the information community—to judge from the results of balloting on the draft of an American National Standard on "Electronic manuscript preparation and markup" (National Information Standards Organization, 1987). This draft standard was opposed only by ASI and a couple of other voting members of NISO, but was endorsed by 37 other members; it is about to be published as an official American Standard this year, thus becoming, if not the law of the land, at least the law of the publishers. This may well entail a nearly intolerable burden on indexers who may be forced to submit their work not only in machine-readable form (which many of them already do quite willingly), but encumbered by a plethora of codes for everything from the start of a new paragraph to a cedilla under a French *c* or the Greek letter *alpha*.

If authors will be actively encouraged by publishers to produce their own indexes by merely tagging so-called "significant" words in their text, this may result in diminishing demand for professionally compiled indexes—and the production of "desktop" indexes hardly deserving that name. Yet since such indexes will be cheap and easy to produce, we may experience a variation of Gresham's law, that is, bad indexes driving out good ones.

Now you might ask, do I believe that only human indexing, fallible and inconsistent as we know it to be, will provide the answer to the problems of information retrieval? Or that all work on automation as an aid to information retrieval is doomed to failure? It would certainly be foolish to claim such things. It seems to me that the answer, as so often, lies in the middle: finding the right balance between what machines can and should do, and what human beings can do best—always keeping in mind that machines can recognize and manipulate *symbols*, but that only human beings can recognize *meaning*, including that which is not explicitly expressed by symbols. This is, of course, easier said than done, and no one, least of all myself, has as yet a good recipe for achieving such a well-balanced state of affairs. But that is true for almost any global problem mankind is faced with. If no good or even acceptable solutions have been found so far for such problems, information retrieval and indexing are in good company, and we need not be ashamed of the fact that, despite so much technological and scientific progress, no panacea is in sight. Polyanna-like prognostications based on ignorance will not get us to the Promised Land of information retrieval. Maybe we still need to wander another forty years in the desert of inadequate methods and faulty systems before we are allowed to even see the Promised Land of indexing from afar.

Meanwhile, we must be content with building up our knowledge piece by piece, like colored pebbles that ultimately form a beautiful mosaic and reveal a full picture. Such knowledge will inevitably have to come from future contributions to the literature of indexing.

The Future of Indexing Literature

Enough said on the kind of contributions we need less of in indexing literature, or even none of. What, then, should be the directions of future research into the theory and practice of indexing? The difficult task of finding the golden mean between machines and human beings has been mentioned, in the spirit of one of the pioneers of the information revolution, Norbert Wiener, who wrote on "the human use of human beings" (Wiener, 1954). While this quotation may be mainly relevant for indexers, who make information retrievable, we also need to know more about the use other human beings are making of our products.

We are still largely ignorant about the amount of use, if any, that is made of indexes, what kind and type of index entries are most useful, and which are little used or not used at all, and hence the making of them is a waste of time and energy on both ends of the chain. Are indexes in printed form used the same way as those presented on a CRT screen? If not (as we suspect, but do not really know), why not?

We need more reports on the failures and shortcomings of PC software for indexing, not in order to pillory or ridicule their inventors and designers (who probably act in good faith when concocting their programs, yet do not pay enough attention to possible mishaps and omission of necessary features), but in order to advance the state of knowledge in that field, and to produce better, simpler, and more user-friendly programs.

We also need more studies on the economics of computer-aided indexing. Most indexers, working alone and not backed by commercial enterprises, can ill afford to change their equipment every time manufacturers come up with a new and more powerful machine, making the software acquired only a year or two ago obsolete because the new machine is incompatible with it. What will be the impact of this phenomenon on the pricing of indexes? Will humanly produced indexes carrying a higher price tag force publishers to publish books without indexes even more often than now, or will they turn to machine-produced indexes of little value? Will those who depend vitally on good and thorough indexing have to accept such indexes? These questions already take us out of the realm of knowledge versus ignorance and into the shaky business of futurology, and my crystal ball is as clouded as anyone else's. Yet of one thing we can be sure: there will be indexes, and there will be those who will write about them, thus contributing to the literature of indexing, which will, in turn, require another literature survey on ASI's 25th birthday in 1993, when, as we all hope, we will have a little more knowledge and a little less ignorance.

Notes

1. Bradford's Law of Scattering states that about 1/3 of the articles on a subject appear in a small number n of journals devoted to that subject; another 1/3 in n^2 journals on other, but related subjects; and 1/3 will be scattered among n^3 journals not normally concerned with the subject. S. C. Bradford was a chemist and director of the Science Museum Library in London during the 1930s.

2. "To index a book, you need to perform these basic steps: 1. Atomize: remove all punctuation, capital letters, apostrophized endings, etc. and put each word in the book on a separate line. 2. Unique: remove all duplicate words. 3. Sort: sort the resulting list of words. 4. Boring: remove 'boring' parts of speech like 'and', 'the', 'but', etc. 5. Page: assign page numbers to the remaining words of interest."

References

Dyson, Freeman J. *Infinite in All Directions*. New York: Harper & Row: 1988.

Luhn, Hans Peter. *Keyword in Context Index for Technical Literature (KWIC index)*. Yorktown Heights, NY: IBM; 1959.

Reprinted in *American Documentation* 9: 288-295; 1960.

National Information Standards Organization (NISO Z39). *Electronic Manuscript: Preparation and Markup*. Gaithersburg, MD: NISO; 1987. (Z39.59-198X).

Polonskaya, O. R. (Logico-Semantic Connectors of the English Language as Formal Indicators of Coherent Text.) *Nauchno-Tekhnicheskaya Informatsiya*. Series 2 (6): 19-22; 1986. In Russian.

Pountain, Dick. Sorting Out the Sorts. *Byte* 12 (8): 275-276, 278, 280; July 1987. Reviewed in *ASI Newsletter* (84): 10; Nov.-Dec. 1987.

Salton, Gerard. Historical Note: The Past Thirty Years in Information Retrieval. *Journal of the American Society for Information Science* 38: 375-380; 1987.

Swanson, Don R. Historical Note: Information Retrieval and the Future of an Illusion. *Journal of the American Society for Information Science* 39: 92-98; 1988.

Weinberg, Bella H. *Word Frequency and Automatic Indexing*. New York: School of Library Service, Columbia University; 1981. (D.L.S. thesis).

Wellisch, Hans H. Some Vital Statistics of Abstracting and Indexing. *International Classification* 7: 135-139; 1980.

Wellisch, Hans H. Vital Statistics on Abstracting and Indexing Revisited. *International Classification* 12: 11-16; 1985.

Wiener, Norbert. *The Human Use of Human Beings: Cybernetics and Society*. 2nd ed. Garden City, NY: Doubleday; 1954.

Book Indexing Principles and Standards: Introduction to the Theme

Most members of the American Society of Indexers are book indexers. The complexity of book indexing and the superior intelligence required of those analyzing the contents of books is often unappreciated by publishers, and the fact that we have quite a few publishers in attendance bodes well for the status of our field.

The American Society of Indexers has formulated criteria for the evaluation of indexes, and gives an award for the best book index of the year, funded by the H. W. Wilson Company (which also gave us shopping bags for our conference). The first time I served as a judge for the Wilson Award, it was at the office of Dorothy Thomas, then President of the American Society of Indexers. We have worked together on judging for this committee several times. In some cases, I have been able to convince her that the index I thought was best should get the prize; but I shall never forget the year I thought the index to a computer manual was deserving of the award, but Dorothy insisted no—because it was missing the word "menu." It became clear to me that Ms. Thomas is a woman of principle, and that is why I asked her to deal with the principles of indexing. She asked that the scope of the topic be expanded to include standards.

Dorothy Thomas *wrote her first index in 1960, for a law book called* Dynamics of the Patent System. *Since then, she has written indexes in many fields—some single volume, some multivolume, some for serials. Ms. Thomas does most of her work in legal indexing, and considers her most important work to be the book-length index to* The Law of Government Contracts *(nine volumes and supplements). She was Senior Editor for the sciences for the* Academic American Encyclopedia Index, *and has also published several articles about indexing. Dorothy Thomas is a long-time member of the American Society of Indexers, a member of its Board, and was President of ASI in 1983-84. She is also a member of many other professional organizations, and for more than ten years, produced and moderated a public affairs radio program. She has traveled extensively and owns her own business, the Dorothy Thomas Company.*

B.H.W.

Book Indexing Principles and Standards

Dorothy Thomas

It is a privilege to be here at this, the 20th Annual Meeting of the American Society of Indexers (ASI).

Before I talk about book indexing, it is necessary to say a word about the membership of ASI. The members are not a homogeneous group. The only tie that binds them is indexing. The majority of the members are free-lance indexers—independent contractors who do indexing on a regular basis for one or more publishers or other private or public organizations. Individually, they do anywhere from a few indexes a year to more than 40 or 50 a year. The next major group of ASI members is composed of librarians, who may do some or a great deal of indexing as part of their full-time work, or do indexing as an occasional part-time project. Another group includes teachers of library science and related subjects. Some of these people do an index infrequently, others do only a small number per year. Still another group is database constructors. And then we have people who work with large, ongoing hard copy serial indexes or on-line databases for private organizations or the government.

The number of book indexes produced each year has increased steadily; their size and form have changed dramatically, and the quality is still very uneven. Databases are well established, but their form and retrieval problems are still not wholly resolved.

Much of the increase and change in book indexing has occurred since 1982, with the advent of wordprocessors and personal computers. The drudgery of hand-written indexes has given way to the aches and pains resulting from sitting in front of a small screen for hours on end. Ergonomic problems notwithstanding, indexing as a profession is growing and becoming less of an esoteric activity. While it is still necessary, at times, to explain how one writes an index, more and more people are familiar with the indexing process and with some of the terms of the art.

Text writing has long been recognized as an art. It is a personal form of expression, a creation of unique style governed by accepted principles of language usage. Indexing is also a form of writing in that indexers create terms and a new order for concepts expressed in a work; they do not merely extract the words. The

Association of American Publishers has accepted the statement that indexers are writers.

Searching or research—the process of information retrieval from a print or electronic product, as in a book index or electronic database—is another art. The Saracevic study just published has concluded that searching is ". . . an art and a very imprecise art at that" [1].

Indexing, a form of writing—the link or interface between a written document and searching—is also an art [2]. It does not lend itself to standardization because the variables are so numerous and critical. Every book is different. We can talk about an art as the subject of theories, principles, style or form, but not standardization.

An illustration of the art of indexing is that the style or form of indexes written by a particular indexer are as recognizable as the work of any fine artist [3]. That is, of course, if the index has not been altered by a copy-editor in a publishing house who is more dedicated to an established style and form—regardless of the needs of the text—than to the content of the index and its responsiveness to the text or the precision of retrieval.

The movement toward computer-generated automatic indexing with a fixed cap on the number of entries is neither art nor science, but a mechanical short-shrifting of scholarship. The explanation that economic considerations are the driving force for this form of indexing is understandable, but serves no one—not the author, not the publisher, and certainly not the end-user.

Authors As Do-It-Yourself Indexers

There will always be a demand by authors, and some publishers, for professional indexers to write so-called hand-made indexes. They may be produced on a computer, but they are not automatic indexes.

No author writes to have his work diminished by inadequate indexing. Authors of trade books, or of scientific and legal works write only a few books in the course of a lifetime. They are, therefore, anxious for the best index to reflect their massive writing effort. The fate of a book may affect the entire career and economic future of an author. It is no wonder that authors fight with editors over indexing; sometimes they fight with indexers.

Like it or not, however, authors are beginning to take over indexing themselves, and more indexes will be author-written and author-edited in the future. Authors will not buy indexing software. Their word processing programs, such as WordPerfect,

XYWrite, and Multimate, have indexing features. Some authors will write tolerable indexes; others will destroy their own work.

Standards and Principles of Indexing

A major problem relating to standards and principles of indexing is the lack of conformity or agreement on the *language* of indexing, i.e., the terms of art. General acceptance of terms of art for indexing is absent.

Yet another problem is that each document indexed requires a separate design, with specific requirements. Standards require uniformity, but books are wholly individual. There are more exceptions than rules. Additionally, each subject or form of document must be reckoned with individually if a standard is to be developed. Wellisch lists more than thirty disciplines covered by indexing services [4].

Form and style may also be controlling elements in the standards of an index. Much depends on who is setting those standards. These are truly standards because they are fixed rules, for example, the number of characters to a line, the number of lines to a page, and typography.

But that does not say that there are not effective and important principles governing indexing. First, however, we must deal with the problem of language.

The Language of Indexing: Invention Run Rampant

The definition of *words of art* is "words used in a technical sense; words scientifically fit to carry the sense assigned them [5]."

Would that the indexing profession could agree on terms so that the members of the profession could understand each other. The entire indexing community is not *au courant* with every newly created term. The members have no regularized means of finding out when, where, and how a given term was invented. We are without a dictionary of terms, and every glossary of indexing is incomplete. In geopolitical terms, we are like a country without a national language, and as a result, we are not unified in our profession, and our public image is fuzzy.

The inability of indexers to communicate with each other on common ground, to understand and exchange information without having to define terms, is distressing and has exclusionary effects. If, for example, you do not know that "subject access system" is another term for *index*, you are an outsider, though you may be the most gifted indexer in the world.

The average indexer can hardly keep up with the changes in terms while meeting his or her deadlines. Granted, many of these changes are in response to new technology and research. A great many, however, are meaningful but futile attempts to grab at solutions for retrieval problems stemming from inadequate indexing. Some people in indexing know some of the new terms; few know all of them. It is an absolute Tower of Babel, unrelieved by a regularly updated reference publication.

To establish principles without a standard language and have them accepted is next to impossible. Furthermore, the absence of a common language makes principles of indexing difficult to describe.

Terms Compared

A comparison of sources of indexing terminology—the National Information Standards Organization's (NISO) Standard Z39.4 (1984 edition) [6], *Subject Access Systems* [7] by Milstead, *Indexing and Searching in Perspective* [8] by Brenner and Saracevic, the criteria for the Wilson Award [9] and the Wheatley Medal [10], *The Chicago Manual of Style* [11] (the Bible of the publishing industry) and a few terms which I have picked up from highly respected indexers with whom I have worked through the years—gives a reasonably clear picture of the problem.

For example: An *index* can be called a (1) *database*, (2) *file*, (3) *index*, or (4) *subject access system*.

For the first line of an index, there is a choice of a minimum of six terms. In alphabetical order, they are: (1) *access point*, (2) *entry*, (3) *index entry*, (4) *heading*, (5) *main heading*, or (6) *subject heading*.

For the single line under the first line of an index, there is a choice of at least three terms: (1) *subhead*, (2) *subentry*, or (3) *modifier*.

For all the lines that follow under any of the above—access point, entry, index entry, heading, main heading, or subject heading, there is a choice of at least five terms: (1) *array*, (2) *file*, (3) *list*, (4) *subheads*, or (5) *record*.

The term *page references* is still used, but is often supplanted by the word *locator*, which is more generalized.

The term *permutation* has changed its meaning in recent years. It is now quite specific in definition, meaning the various forms or turnings an index entry can take. Twenty-five years ago, it was a synonym for *indents*. It has been replaced by *indents* (1,2,or 3) or *levels* (1,2,or 3).

About the only term of art that seems to have resisted the exercise in synonymity is *cross-reference*. It is the single term that was found in every set of guidelines or principles examined. *Syndetic structure*, an elegant alliteration meaning connecting structure, is not a new term, but is only now coming into common use.

Activity on the Language Issue

Well, everyone isn't standing still on this language issue. The American Society for Information Science (ASIS) has embarked on a project to establish a thesaurus for information science, which will include indexing terms of art. This project is ready for final approval, but between the date of final approval and the final publication date of the thesaurus, a substantial amount of time will pass. This gives ASI time to get its own house in order and present to the ASIS task force indexing terms of art—*our choices* for the terms of art.

Believe me, ASI doesn't need the ASIS thesaurus. We need a good dictionary or glossary published by us and distributed by us, to every teacher in every school of library and information service, to every editor in every publishing house and university press—including the University of Chicago Press, publishers of *The Chicago Manual of Style*; to every member of ASI; and also published in the journals of ASIS, SLA (Special Libraries Association, MLA (Medical Library Association), and ALA (American Library Association). The glossary should be regularly reviewed and revised. Furthermore, it should include the criteria for the Wilson Award, which is as good a set of indexing principles as can be found today.

Style and Format Confused with Principles

Too often instructions as to the *style* of an index, that is, the position of headings, the number of ems or characters for indents, the number of columns on a page, and type faces are taken for indexing principles. A publishing company will give an indexer a small (or large) booklet, or a set of pages called the XYZ Company Indexing Instructions. These documents are almost always standard style instructions or "house" style instructions and guides. Only occasionally do they include principles of indexing.

Principles of Indexing

The principles of indexing are the closest we can come to standards. In the same way that writing is governed by grammar and usage, so indexing is governed by principles of clarity and accuracy. Not a year goes by without an article on what makes a good index, the criteria for the Wheatley Award, or other guides being published that include a statement of principles. More than half a dozen such articles have appeared in *The Indexer* during the last ten years; most of them repeat the same principles [12]. Essentially, principles of indexing are based on common sense and accurate, careful, consistent writing. But the principles of indexing are not fixed—they can and should be adjusted in the interest of clarity and ease of searching for those exceptional situations where the usual procedure cannot be followed.

There is general agreement on the principles of indexing when the literature is examined [13]. Briefly, these principles are as follows:

1. The needs of the user must be primarily served.

2. The index should reflect the text. It should not be the author's addendum to the text, nor should the indexer rewrite or prejudice the text by omissions or additions. (The indexer has a great deal of power, which is not generally recognized.)

3. Alphabetization or any other order used must be accurate.

4. Locators should be both accurate and complete.

5. Index entries should move from the general to the specific. (This is most important in very large indexes, where general headings have numerous subdivisions and cross-references send the user to more specific terms.)

6. Significant items in the text must appear in the index. Decisions must be made about the coverage of such items as chapter headings, tables, and illustrations.

7. Consistency of terms is essential.

8. Cross-references should be used to connect unique language in the text to main headings. There must be enough cross-references to connect related items in the index and to relate out-of-date or idiosyncratic terms in the text to current usage. This is where the indexer's knowledge and experience are significant.

9. Strings of undifferentiated locators should be limited to four. More than that number should be avoided by the use of subheadings, additional major headings, or other devices.

10. An introductory note should be provided if an index requires explanation. It should be clear and well expressed, and it should establish the basis of selection and omission of indexable matter.

11. Abbreviations in the text should be represented in the index both as an abbreviation and under the full expression of the letters,

with one form cross-referenced to the other.

12. Entries beginning with prepositions should be avoided. (For some indexers and, more often, editors, eliminating the preposition as the first word of an entry is nothing short of a crime against humanity. Other indexers and editors drop the preposition in the interest of ease of alphabetization and use an apostrophe. The user "has enough to do concentrating on the descriptive word in the search without being distracted by a disordered array cluttered with prepositions which are ignored in the alphabetization" [14]. The elimination of the preposition is a good tradeoff as it increases the precision of retrieval.)

The Real World of Publishing

Most indexed books are from the social sciences [15]. Though more publishers are involved in the production of such books than other categories of informational works, the problems of creating indexes are essentially the same in all disciplines. Book publishers live in a very high-pressured, nervous, rigid world. There is an arrogance about some editors and others who are responsible for the indexes to the books their companies produce. Sad to say, much of the arrogance comes from ignorance. (Who ever said a copy editor is qualified to be an indexer or index editor?) These people are unreasonably dependent on the indexing guidelines in *The Chicago Manual of Style*. For them, it is a safe haven—the highest authority—the court of last resort for settling indexing questions. It is not the definitive guide, nor does it represent the principles of the American Society of Indexers. There must be communication between the copy editor and the indexer.

Ask any editor in a major publishing house about the American National Standards Institute's Z39.4 (or Z39 as we call it), and they will think you are talking about a new rock group, a new automobile model, or a new sun-block. As much as we publicize the Wilson Award and its criteria, year after year, we reach few of the people in publishing houses who employ indexers. The criteria for the Wilson Award, adapted from the criteria for the British Wheatley Medal, form a very superior set of indexing principles.

The Chicago Manual of Style confers a singular power on the copy editor from which the indexer has no appeal. It is the power of final editing. *The Manual of Style* at Section 18.127 states, "The following suggestions for editing an index are based on the experience of the University of Chicago Press editors, augmented by a checklist that editors at a sister university press shared with us" [16]. (They never asked ASI for its views!) There are nine items in the list; seven recommendations are reasonable and sensible indexing principles having to do with accuracy, consistency, and the like; but two items are clear causes of conflict between some editors and indexers.

Item 7 states, "If some entries seem overanalyzed (many sub-heads with only one page reference each), try to combine some of them, and if subheadings are longer and more elaborate than necessary, try and simplify them" [17].

This is the rule that gives rise to undifferentiated references. Reducing subheads so that they are shortened and make a nice neat line without a turnover also takes the heart out of the index and out of the book. Many editors subscribe to the "rule of level 3"— no more than three levels, including main heading and two subheads.

Ask anyone who has been on the Wilson Award committee about the plague of undifferentiated references, which have wrecked more than one excellent index. Judges and end users alike look at six, eight, and even ten undifferentiated references and hold their heads in despair. Entries like this are an insult to the end user, and to the author, whose efforts are never going to be utilized. They are, moreover, a red-ink item to the publisher. Because publishers invariably know so little about indexing, they do not realize that indexes sell books. The cost of an additional page of an index can extend the sales life of a book and bring an increased return on investment.

Item 8 states: "If necessary, delete any trivial items you recognize from your own work on the book. . . . (Be careful here. This can be dangerous. It can also involve you in a great deal more work than you bargained for)" [18].

The best advice would be for the editor to keep his/her hands off the index altogether.

Ethical Standards

Here is an issue for which I have no answer, but since we are talking about standards and principles, we must include the matter of publishers' actions and indexers' ethics. This is the problem.

Indexer Responsibility and Publisher's Requirements
The indexer has an ethical responsibilty to serve the text and the author. The publisher is in a cash-intensive business, requiring a quick turnover on investments. The editor, on instructions from a superior, requires the indexer to cut the index, and delete subheads and other entries, thus creating many entries with undifferentiated

references and shortened, inadequate subheads. Alternatively, the indexer may be required to mention a particular state or city or name in the index, even if the name is not part of indexable text.

In the process, important and unique information in the text that appeared in the original index is buried or lost forever, and the scholarly value of the book is measurably decreased. The indexer's name is not mentioned in the book, but the indexer is left with an uneasy feeling about the loss of index entries and the destruction of the integrity of the index. It's an all too common, not very nice picture.

What should the indexer do in such cases?

The Choices
—Should the indexer attempt to talk to the editor and suggest other ways of getting the index printed in its entirety by reducing the print size or the margins? (That generally does not work.)

—Should the indexer defend the index vigorously, at the risk of losing out on future work from the publisher?

—If the indexer was hired by the author, should the indexer explain to the author that he/she had no control over the final editing?

—Should the indexer give a copy of the full index to the author for the author's own benefit?

—Should the indexer rationalize the problem as being one beyond his/her control and the nature of indexer-publisher relations?

—Or should the indexer not dwell on it, take the payment, and get on with the next job—feelings or no feelings?

This is an issue for which there is no easy answer.

And What of the Future?

The American Society of Indexers had a Committee on Ethics, Standards, and Specifications. In 1974, it issued a set of guidelines and specifications for indexes and indexer-publisher relations. The committee should be reconstituted so that now, some seventeen years later, it can work on indexing principles and ethics as well as the compilation of a dictionary or glossary. There is every reason to believe that such a committee will be successful, and that ASI will meet all the challenges of the future.

References

1. Saracevic, Tefko. A Study of Information Seeking and Retrieving, III. Searchers, Searches, and Overlap. *Journal of the American*

Society for Information Science. 39(3): 197-216; 1988.

2. Knight, G. *Indexing, the Art of* (1979); Tatham, F. H. C. What Is a Good Index? *The Indexer* 8(1): 23-28; April 1972.

3. Tatham, F. H. C. What Is a Good Index?, *The Indexer* 8(1): 23-28; April 1972.

4. Wellisch, Hans H. *Abstracting and Indexing,* 1977-1981. Santa Barbara, CA: Clio Press; 1984: 262.

5. *Black's Law Dictionary.* 5th ed. 1979, p. 1439.

6. American National Standards Institute, *American National Standard for Library and Information Sciences and Related Publishing Practices—Basic Criteria for Indexes.* ANSI Z39.4-1984: 7-9.

7. Milstead, Jessica L. *Subject Access Systems: Alternatives in Design.* Orlando, FL: Academic Press; 1984.

8. Brenner, Everett; Saracevic, Tefko. *Indexing and Searching In Perspective.* Philadelphia, PA: National Federation of Abstracting and Information Services; 1985.

9. American Society of Indexers, *Register,*1986: 22-23.

10. Hamilton, Geoffrey. How to Recognize a Good Index. *The Indexer* 10(2):53; Oct. 1976.

11. University of Chicago Press. *The Chicago Manual of Style* (13th ed.) 1982: 511-556.

12. Hamilton, Geoffrey. How to Recognize a Good Index. *The Indexer* 10(2): 49-53; Oct. 1976; Harrod, L. M. Official Guidance on Book Indexes. *The Indexer* 10(3): 124-130; April 1977; Harrod, L. M. and Piggott, Mary. The British Standards Institute and Its Recommendations for Indexes. *The Indexer* 10(4): 186-191; Oct. 1977; Hall, Brenda M. Getting the Index Right: Roles and Responsibilities. *The Indexer* 13(3): 166-171; Apr. 1983; Anderson, M. D. An Indexer's Suggestions to (Some) Publishers. *The Indexer* 14(3): 190; Apr. 1985; Vickers, John A. Index, How Not To. *The Indexer* 15(3): 163-166; Apr. 1987; Tousignaut, Dwight R. Indexing: Old Methods, New Concepts. *The Indexer* 15(4): 197-204; Oct. 1987.

13. *Supra* nn. 4,12.

14. Thomas, Dorothy. Law Book Indexing. In: *Indexing Specialized Formats and Subjects.* H. Feinberg, ed. Metuchen, NJ: Scarecrow Press; 1983: 171.

15. Seal, Alan. Indexes from a User's Viewpoint. *The Indexer* 14(2): 111-113; Oct. 1984.

16. *The Chicago Manual (Supra* n.11) 550.

17. 16 Id. 551.

18. Ibid.

Indexing Software: Introduction to the Theme

The computer has revolutionized indexing practice as it has many other professions. Seventy-five percent of respondents to a survey, the results of which were published in the March (1988) issue of the American Society of Indexers Newsletter, *use computers. Many publishers now receive machine-readable indexes. The statistics reported in the same issue of the* ASI Newsletter *indicate that over 50 percent of indexers submit their indexes either on diskette or by modem. We expect that soon, indexes will even be generically coded for typesetting; the American Society of Indexers will shortly issue Hugh Maddocks' booklet* Generic Markup of Electronic Index Manuscripts.

The acknowledged expert on indexing software is Linda Fetters, who has published two editions of a guide to such software through ASI and who writes "The Electronic Shoebox" column for the ASI Newsletter.

Linda K. Fetters *is a graduate of San Diego State University, and of the Graduate School of Library and Information Science, University of Texas at Austin. She is a free-lance indexer, technical writer, and records management consultant. Previous positions include Staff Writer, Xanthus Corporation; Assistant Librarian for Technical Services at the Texas Medical Association Memorial Library; and Information Analyst at Balcones Computer Corporation. Since 1982, she has written a column on indexing software for the* ASI Newsletter, *and has published several other articles related to computer-aided indexing in major library and information science periodicals.*

B.H.W.

Indexing Software

Linda K. Fetters

Introduction

Before the widespread availability of microcomputers, indexing software could be found only on mainframe computers in universities and large businesses. Individuals outside these environments had no access to computerized indexing.

Now there are indexing programs to meet every need and style. Indeed, the software is changing the way we organize information, sometimes even eliminating the "middleman" indexer from the process.

Types of Software

Indexing software can be classified into two groups. In the first group, an indexer controls what terms and phrases go into the index. In the second group, the software controls what goes into the index. As you might expect, there is some overlap between the two groups.

The *indexer-controlled group* consists of three categories of programs:

1. *Stand-alone indexing programs*, for back-of-the-book index production;

2. *Built-in* or *embedded indexing programs*, that generate indexes from terms embedded in machine-readable text files;

3. *Hypertext programs*, which link information in one file to related information in another file.

The *software-controlled group* consists of the following three categories:

1. *Text retrieval* or *text database programs*, which, like online databases, allow for the retrieval of words, phrases, or combinations of words or phrases in machine-readable text files;

2. *Automatic indexing software*, which generates an index based on human-produced lists of terms to be included or excluded;

3. *Expert systems* (artificial intelligence), which perform work guided by rules based on human experience.

These types of indexing software can be viewed as aids to our profession or threats to our livelihood. We shall examine each category and then determine what effect it has on indexers.

Human-Controlled Indexing

In this group of software, the indexer determines what index entries are input, or in the case of hypertext, which documents are linked together.

Stand-alone Indexing Programs

This category of indexing software has come a long way in the past ten years. In the early 1980s, there were no commercially available indexing programs. Several indexers had commissioned programs for their own use and offered them for sale, but until the IBM PC standardized the microcomputer market, there were too many incompatible operating systems for any of these programs to become successful or widespread in use (Fetters, 1988).

After Compugramma released its Micro Indexing System for the IBM PC in early 1983, the indexing software market began to grow. The Foxon-Maddocks Index Preparation System, which had been written for the Radio Shack Model II, was converted to the IBM PC in 1984. That same year, the PC-version of MACREX appeared. Now there are at least eleven programs available for the IBM PC family and its compatibles and clones.

These specialized programs, used mostly by professional indexers, editors at publishing houses, and some libraries, enable the indexer to type indexing phrases he/she has selected into the program, which then alphabetizes, formats, and prints the index. These programs typically reduce the time previously required to index a document by the manual method by 30-50% or more.

Built-in or Embedded Indexing Software

Another category of software that performs virtually the same functions as the stand-alone category is built-in or embedded indexing software. Unlike stand-alone software, however, this type of index-generating program works only with a document in machine-readable form created by a specific word processor or electronic publishing program.

These kinds of programs are commonly used in technical publications departments of companies that produce computer hardware or software manuals, or by smaller publishers who use desktop or electronic publishing systems.

Indexers who use built-in indexing software go through the same process as in indexing manually or with stand-alone programs. They must analyze the document and decide on index entries. But instead of typing these entries on cards or into a separate progam, they either mark the entries directly in the text file, or type them into special indexing windows in the text file, which then disappear from the screen, as they contain "hidden text."

After the index terms are embedded, the programs gather together all the embedded index entries, attach page numbers, alphabetize, and format the index according to a pre-determined style. The better programs in this category, such as the Interleaf Technical Publishing System, give the indexer control over the sorting of unusual terms and symbols, and also allow for as many as five levels of subheadings.

The main problem in indexing with these programs is that it is difficult to see how the index is shaping up as you work through each chapter. You typically do not know what problems may arise until you see the final, formatted index. You may then discover, after you have made all the entries, that you have scattered terms, spelled them differently, or phrased headings inconsistently. Then you have to go back through each chapter, find the offending index entries, make corrections, and regenerate the index.

The advantage of such programs is that once the index entries are correct, you do not have to check all the page references when revisions are made. You simply embed index entries for any new material added to the document and re-run the index program to automatically change all the page numbers that are affected.

Whether or not major publishing houses will use this type of software or require indexers to work with such programs is unknown. My own experience is that more and more of my technical publications clients are asking me to perform this type of indexing, either giving me their text files and asking me to embed the terms directly into them, or asking for a printed index in page number order to be inserted in the text files by an employee of theirs who is familiar with the software.

Hypertext

Hypertext is the current buzzword in new wave software. Unlike any other software, it can best be compared with database management and text retrieval software. Hypertext was first developed on mainframes and minis in the 1960s and 1970s, and has only recently appeared on microcomputers (Franklin, 1988; Smith, 1988). Apple Computer brought this variety of software to the public's attention in 1987 with its HyperCard product. A similar program for the IBM PC family is Guide from Owl International.

Strictly speaking, hypertext programs are not indexing programs at all. In fact, they remove traditional indexes from the picture completely. Hypertext databases consist of a collection of full-text articles or other information in machine-readable form, stored on a hard disk or some other medium, such as optical disk or CD-ROM. The owner of the collection establishes links between related files or documents in the database so that a user can follow a pre-established path from one document to another related document without referring to an external index.

For example, suppose you are sitting at a computer terminal reading an article about expert systems, and you come across a reference to automatic indexing. By selecting a "button" that has been embedded in the text, you can go directly to another document within the collection that contains the referenced document with related information. That article also contains "buttons" that lead you to other related information.

As opposed to a search in a printed index or online database for articles on a topic, a hypertext system has been pre-indexed in a way that brings related articles directly to your screen, after you identify one document of interest. Of course, the main limitation of such a system is that you can only find information that has been included in the hypertext database. Hypertext guru, Ted Nelson, has set the ambitious goal of converting all existing information to hypertext form in his Xanadu system. He plans to make the Xanadu system available to millions of users (Franklin, 1988).

Software-Controlled Indexing

In this group, the software controls the indexing process with a minimum of human intervention.

Text Retrieval Software

Text retrieval or text database management programs are considered a type of indexing software because they "index" every significant word in a machine-readable text file. Users can search for specific words or phrases using Boolean search techniques, just as they would in online databases such as those available through BRS and DIALOG.

These programs are particularly useful when word association or proximity is important. Another advantage of this type of program over a printed index is that when you perform a search, you can instantly verify its accuracy by displaying the retrieved sentences or paragraphs.

Some of these programs require a great deal of preparation of the text files before they can be used. Others require no preparation of the text; rather, they read the specified files, "crunch" all the words, and create a separate index containing pointers to all significant words in the specified text files. Yet other programs require neither preparation nor an external index. They read through each word in the file, like a sophisticated search function in a word processor, and display the requested combination of terms. They take longer to locate a word or phrase or search statement than indexed systems, but they don't require any advance preparation time.

These programs are useful for organizations that have large numbers of files already on a hard disk or CD-ROM, with no way to locate information in those files. Even libraries that do not have enough staff members to devote time to indexing large collections of materials are finding it attractive to store unindexed materials on hard disks (Holland, 1985) and to use a text retrieval program to recall the information. Several text retrieval programs also work with text stored on CD-ROM.

Text retrieval programs vary a great deal in the features they offer in addition to the basic retrieval function. Some contain database management functions which allow maintenance of mailing lists or bibliographic files and automatic formatting of such files. Other programs in this group offer "cut and paste" capabilities, allowing you to find text in one file and copy it into another file, even if the text was created by a different program.

What effects will text retrieval programs have on traditional indexing? In his look at trends in subject indexing, Lancaster (1980) speculated that free-text searching will replace conventional subject indexing in online databases. According to him, studies show that natural language searching retrieves information as well as searches based on controlled vocabularies, and the need for indexing is declining rapidly.

Lancaster's ideas notwithstanding, there's no reason why a controlled vocabulary cannot be superimposed on text files to improve search precision in the use of text retrieval programs. In a project performed for a state agency, I abstracted thousands of pages of legislative committee hearings and prepared them for use with a text retrieval program. In the abstracts, I used the language of the original documents as much as possible; however, I also added terms from a small thesaurus I constructed while abstracting the materials, and gave the thesaurus, along with a manual for the system, to the people who would be searching the text database.

For more information on these types of programs, you may want to review the December 1987 issue of *Database* magazine, which is devoted to this subject.

Automatic Indexing and Expert Systems

The distinction between the last two groups of indexing software is rapidly blurring.

Indexers, linguists, and computer scientists have been trying to teach computers to index documents for a long time, at least since the early 1960s. One of our colleagues, W. Bruce Croft, will update us on automatic indexing technology this afternoon.

Harold Borko concluded from his experiments with automatic indexing that the computer could not be programmed to compile a usable index based on single words or even multiple-word phrases. After much work with term exclusion and computer selection of word pairs, he finally decided that fully automated indexing was not possible at that time (Borko, 1970).

With the advent of artifical intelligence and expert systems, however, we may expect some progress in this area. In an article on computerized indexing, Kevin Jones postulates just that:

> Expert Systems are intended to capture human expertise and encapsulate it within a computer system. Unlike most earlier programming, the new technique is deliberately designed to cope with uncertain areas of human knowledge. There seems to be general agreement that the indexing process is poorly understood: therefore, Expert Systems may eventually be able to elucidate this knowledge (Jones, 1986, 12).

The American Petroleum Institute (Brenner, 1984) has already designed an expert-like system for automatically indexing abstracts for the API database. (We shall hear from Mr. Brenner this afternoon as well.) Using a thesaurus developed over twenty years of indexing, the program matches natural language in abstracts with terms in the thesaurus. It then prints the abstract along with the identified index terms, showing where the terms appear in the abstract. A human editor then checks for missed terms.

API's goal is not only to cut down on the cost of indexing, but also to use this program to increase the efficiency of searching their database. The expert system would match the searcher's natural language statements with terms in the thesaurus, converting the natural language into an efficient search statement.

There seems to be little doubt that automated indexing procedures will gradually reduce the need for human indexers in the production of online databases.

Computers and Indexers

What are the implications of all these types of indexing software for indexers?

Despite the fact that automatic indexing may reduce opportunities for indexers in some areas, it seems from my own experience that there is currently a great deal of interest in indexing techniques in the business community, especially in how businesses can use the various types of indexing software to help keep their business records organized.

Records management is a fertile field for indexers, and some text retrieval programs are well suited for managing computerized information, or for creating online indexes to paper filing systems.

Indexers can also play useful roles in converting paper documents to machine-readable files for use with either text retrieval programs or hypertext systems. Even though text retrieval systems can be used without the enrichment of index terms, indexers can create thesauri for such databases and add the controlled vocabulary to the text files to increase search precision.

Hypertext systems seem especially well-suited for indexers who are used to tracking their way through myriad relationships within documents. Hypertext systems will undoubtedly bloom in the academic environment where departments can set up course-related document structures to assist students with their research (Smith, 1988).

As far as back-of-the-book indexing is concerned, it seems that both stand-alone and embedded indexing programs will continue to provide the best methods of production, depending on publishers' needs.

Rather than reducing the opportunities for indexers, these advances in indexing software create a whole new realm of possibilities for those who are bold enough to explore them.

References

Borko, Harold. Experiments in Book Indexing by Computer. *Information Storage and Retrieval* 6: 5-16; 1970.

Brenner, E. H.; Lucey, J. H.; Martinez, C. L.; Meleka, Adel. American Petroleum Institute's Machine-Aided Indexing and Searching Project. *Science and Technology Libraries* 5: 49-62; 1984.

Fetters, Linda K. Progress in Indexing Software. *Online* 12:116-123; 1988.

Franklin, Carl. Hypertext on the PC: Guide, Version 1. *Database* 11: 95-100; 1988.

Holland, Maurita Peterson. ZyINDEX: Full Text Retrieval Power. *Online* 9: 38-42; 1985.

Ingebretsen, Dorothy. Information Management Software—A Selected Bibliography. *Database* 10: 27-34; 1987.

Jones, Kevin P. Getting Started in Computerized Indexing. *Indexer* 15: 9-13; 1986.

Lancaster, F. Wilfred. Trends in Subject Indexing from 1957 to 2000. In: Taylor, Peter J., ed. *New Trends in Documentation and Information*: Proceedings of the International Federation for Documentation (FID) 39th Congress; 1978 September 25-38; Edinburgh, Scotland. London, England: Aslib; 1980: 223-233. (FID Publication no. 566).

Smith, Karen E. Hypertext—Linking to the Future. *Online* 12: 32-40; 1988.

Database Design: Introduction to the Theme

The topics treated up to this point represent the heart of ASI activity; the authoritative bibliographies on indexing, book indexing standards, and guides to indexing software emanate from the American Society of Indexers or its members. Database design is, however, a subject of interest to many communities, and it has a vast literature. ASI membership is not limited to book indexers, and includes many who work for serial abstracting and indexing services and even some who design databases.

Many database designers with only a computer background often reinvent the wheel and could learn a great deal from the literature of indexing and library-information science. The person I invited to discuss database design, Dr. Jessica Milstead, is an expert on the organization of information, who wrote a very thought-provoking book on the tradeoffs in database design (Subject Access Systems: Alternatives in Design). (*History will show, however, that her greatest claim to fame is the fact that she was my cataloging teacher at Columbia University!*)

Dr. Jessica Milstead *started her own consulting firm in late 1986, offering services in thesaurus and index design and development. Before that she was Vice President/Editorial Director of NewsBank, inc. She has held other positions in industry and in academe.*

Recently, she has been working on contracts with both government and private industry, ranging from assisting in development of an information system to support the licensing application for a high-level nuclear waste repository to a cumulative index for a children's magazine.

Dr. Milstead's most recent book, Subject Access Systems *(Orlando: Academic Press, 1984), won the ASIS Information Science Book of the Year Award in 1985 and was also a runner-up for an ASI indexing award. She chairs the American Society of Indexers' Constitution Committee and is also very active in ASIS.*

B. H. W.

Database Design: Indexing Applications

Jessica L. Milstead

Introduction

The principles of database design have been fairly well known for a number of years, but until recently, computer resource requirements have limited development of databases of meaningful size to larger mini- and mainframe systems. Today, however, personal computers have become more powerful, and database software which can handle realistic volumes within their limitations is available. It is now appropriate for indexers to consider using such software to develop databases for index production, and to broaden the scope of their services accordingly.

The purpose of this paper is to provide background to aid indexers in deciding whether a database approach is more appropriate than use of specialized indexing or bibliographic software for a given task. For situations where the database approach is chosen, guidance is offered in issues relating to design of the database, followed by information on use of software packages. The discussion is limited to smaller databases and database software of the sort that can be implemented on a personal computer with a hard disk drive. Knowledge-based systems and hypertext are not considered; these are still in their infancy, especially at the PC level.

First, though, we need to ask how a database is different from an index. The general answer is that an index, like a library card catalog or telephone directory, *is* a database, of a very limited type. Fidel (1987), for example, defines a database as "a store of data about a selected part of the real world that is intended to be used for particular purposes."

Even though this general definition does not limit databases to implementation on computers, only by means of computers is it possible to make intensive use of the information stored in a database, and this paper is limited to databases which are stored and processed by computer. In fact, the whole point of database design today is to organize information in such a way that it can be accessed in a number of different ways and used for a much wider variety of purposes than in the past. This flexibility requires use of computers.

Consideration of some examples will make clear the differences between the conventional index and the modern database. When conventional indexing techniques are used, each type of information user has his or her own data store. A library will have a catalog of books and a file of borrower information. When a borrower has checked out a book, a third file connecting the two (i.e., showing the relationship) is maintained, but it contains limited information, and is usually accessible from only one point of view. If the file is arranged by date due, for example, it is not possible to determine which books a given borrower has taken out. If the library develops a database, however, complete connections between borrower information and book information can be made, making it easy to place a hold on a book, to determine where a requested book may be, or to track borrower interests. To take the example further, in an academic library, the borrower information may even be part of, or drawn from, a general database on students and faculty of the university.

In a publishing milieu, the fulfillment department has the information in the publisher's catalog from which to work, while the acquisitions editors maintain files on authors and prospective authors. Most likely, there will never be a connection between these two files. When a database is used, however, all the needed information can be maintained, permitting such queries as the past sales of a prospective author's books, or the status of the production stream for a particular work, to be answered readily.

But how does this apply to the real-life indexer who is not likely to be automating either a library's or a publisher's files? Certainly, in preparing a back-of-the-book index for one-time publication there is little relationship, and for this kind of application a special-purpose indexing program will serve the need admirably. Similarly, a bibliographic-type index, such as a one-time printed periodical index, can be produced using one of the specialized bibliography programs which can produce indexes on a variety of data elements.

As soon as the needs become more sophisticated, however, the desirability of database organization becomes evident. Take a newspaper, for example. The conventional print-on-paper newspaper index offers only subject access—frequently very broad subjects, but this is not a necessary condition. But consider all the other points of interest: specific subjects, individual writers and columns, extent and types of illustrations, names in bewildering variety, even the section of the paper in which an item appeared (e.g., local news, which is indicative of the slant of the article), or the relative length of articles (which would facilitate content analysis of the newspaper, i.e., the extent of coverage of a given topic).

A conventional newspaper index cannot readily answer such questions as:

> Are there photographs showing George Bush with Oliver North?
> How much space is given to news of specific parts of the world?
> Did Mary McGrory write about the stock market crash?

The number of access points required to answer such questions in a printed index would exceed the limits of practicality.

Any of the following needs may suggest that development of a database is warranted; if several of them are present, this course of action may be highly advisable.

> Expectations of cumulation, updating, or revision;
> Need for report layouts which are not available within a specialized program;
> Need for a variety of types of reports, some of which may not be specifiable at the time of original development;
> Need to query the database for specialized reports or from a variety of points of view.

Comparison of Indexing, Bibliographic, and Database Software

In today's market, an indexer who wishes to use the computer, but who does not plan to develop his or her own software, basically must choose among three types of packages: specialized indexing or bibliographic systems and generalized database systems. (Given the wide choice of other software available today, making indexes with word processing software is not a viable alternative, unless the full text is available for processing in the software. Even then, the limitations of the software should be examined carefully. For instance, cross references and/or continuous paging may not be possible.)

Indexing programs. A wide variety of indexing programs is available today; no generalized database software is likely to improve on them in the applications for which they are designed. In a sense, an indexing program is like a highly specialized database program in which both the fields and the reports are already almost completely defined. All the indexer has to do is a little fine-tuning, and work can begin.

The "database," as defined in the indexing program, is one of heading, subheading, sub-subheading, etc., followed by a locator such as a page reference. The ability to manipulate the information within a record (an index entry) is very limited. For example, while it is possible to show that newspaper articles contain photos by putting "(photo)" at the end of a subheading, one cannot return at a later date and search for all the photos or all illustrated articles on a given topic.

Bibliographic programs. A number of these programs exist; they were originally designed to aid development of bibliographies or library catalogs, but many also permit indexes to be developed automatically. If the content of the index is bibliographic entries, such as newspaper or periodical articles, and the only product is print on paper without extensive updating, this option is well worth examining. The record is similar to that in a hierarchical database, but much of the design is already provided, saving labor at the price of reduced flexibility.

Database systems. Use of a database organization increases the flexibility of a system dramatically. This flexibility, however, comes at a price; it is necessary to put significant resources into defining the database and its elements. Additional resources are then required for definition of reports.

Development of a Database

Definitions. The *record* is the basic organizational element of a database. It consists of all the information about some item, e.g., the bibliographic information for a book or periodical article. A *file* is a group of records, and a *field* or *data element* is an identifiable unit of information within a record (e.g., an author or a title).

Types of organization. Databases are usually organized in one of two ways:

Hierarchical organization is the traditional form. Fields are organized into records and records into files; a database typically consists of a single file. A given data element is part of one record, which is part of one file, and so on. Hierarchical organization is relatively inflexible.

In a *relational* organization, a number of files can be created, and relationships between them defined that make it possible to treat the data much more flexibly.

There is a third type, the *network*, which combines features of the hierarchical and relational organizations, but this type is not very important to a designer using available DBMS software on a PC, and it will not be discussed here.

The hierarchical organization is easiest to conceptualize because it matches the kind of organization that is almost unavoidable in a manual system. For example, in a conventional printed index, the index itself is the file, and the record is the individual index entry. This record may contain a number of data elements, such as subject heading, author, title, and bibliographic information in a periodical index.

In a situation where multiple entries of a single type—such as subject—must be made for a single item, the difference between hierarchical and relational organizations is clearly exemplified. No commercially available PC-based DBMS package—at least none that this author has ever seen—permits more than one occurrence of a given field in a record.[1] This means that there is no way to make multiple subject entries in a record.

Using such a package, it is necessary to repeat the bibliographic information in a separate record for each subject term, and for each author, if there is more than one. Most packages permit automatic copying of repetitive information, but any subsequent editing and correction would have to be performed separately on every copy of the information. This brute force approach is not particularly practicable.

With a relational database structure, more effort is required in design, but the above problem can be avoided. For example, in a project recently executed by this author, a subject index to a fourteen-year run of a periodical was prepared using PARADOX software. Authors, titles, bibliographic information, and subjects were each stored in separate files; the records for a given article were connected by the fact that they had the same accession number. If the only purpose had been to produce the subject index, two files would have been sufficient: one of subjects and one of all other information. It seemed wise, however, to provide for possible later production of an author or title index. It was easy to design in this capability at the start; adding it later would have required massive editing or complete rekeying.

A special input form was designed so that it appeared to the operator that all the information about a given item was being

---

[1] There are packages for minicomputers and large micros which have this capability, but these are out of the price range that a single indexer or a small database producer could afford.

keyed into a single record. The system then split the various components into the appropriate files, rejoining them for editing, corrections, and output.

In less conventional situations, where even more flexibility and interconnection are required, the advantages of relational organization are even more evident. The examples below bring this out.

Conceptual design issues. The information in a database can be conceived in three categories: entities, relationships, and attributes. An *entity* is a thing about which information is stored, *relationships* are actions or effects of one entity upon another, and *attributes* are characteristics of either entities or relationships.

In a library database, for instance, both books and borrowers may be entities, with the relationship that borrowers check out (or otherwise access) books. Attributes of books may be such items as author or publication date; attributes of borrowers may be address, identification number, or status.

The distinction between an entity and an attribute is not cut and dried. In the library database, it is reasonable to consider specific books as entities. But for a publisher, the situation is different.

Certainly for fulfillment the book is the entity, but how about for acquisitions editors? For them, it is more reasonable to regard the author or potential author as an entity. This can be handled by considering both books and authors as entities, the relationship being that the book is written by the author.

Clearly, one type of entity in a newspaper database would be articles, but then the situation becomes more complex. Are people entities or attributes? Is the byline of an article or column an attribute ("author"), or is that person a separate entity, standing in the relationship "is author of" to the article? This question might be relatively easily decided in favor of a relationship between entities, but then we come to all the other people who are *mentioned* in articles. Normally they would be considered subjects (attributes) of the article, but the same thing should not be both an entity and an attribute.

Yet, if all people become entities, how are the other subjects of articles to be treated? This paper only poses the question; final decisions on such issues depend on the usage envisioned for the database.

Another example: The *Physicians' Desk Reference* is an important listing of drugs, revised annually. It contains manufacturer-provided descriptions of drugs, with indexes by manufacturer, product name, product category, and generic and chemical names. Two supplements are produced during the year.

Assume that this product is to be made available on CD-ROM with index access similar to that which is presently available.

To keep the example simple, let us assume that the database consists of information *about* the full text, and that a software connection is made to the text inself. Also to keep the example simple, we will ignore the problems of chemical structures and pictures which exist in the present printed product.

The advantages of such a product can include faster access to the information, speedier and more convenient updating, and the ability to print out information on a selected drug as desired.

In analysis, it appears at first that the drug should be treated as the entity; its attributes are its various names as well as the name of its manufacturer.

The design questions quickly become more complicated, however. Is each manufacturer's version of a particular drug an entity, or is a generic formulation the entity, regardless of manufacturer? In a product such as this one, the answer is probably the first alternative, since manufacturers provide the data; the publication is a compendium of information about named drugs, not about generic formulations. The various names (generic, chemical, etc.) become attributes.

Once design has gone this far, however, it quickly becomes evident that the value of this database need not be limited to production of the printed publication, important though that is. If corporations are also defined as entities, with the relationship of "manufactures" to specific drugs, the database can become the foundation of the entire process of preparing the publication. Records for manufacturers which can be used in the process of gathering the information can be included.

The process of updating then becomes one of generating update requests to manufacturers and adding or deleting drug names and manufacturers; one or more queries then organizes the data for the various reports (including the publication, whether on CD-ROM or paper).

The analysis of the various types of information, and the relationships among them, to be included in the database will have a strong effect on the quality of the final product.

Content control. In the database environment, it is important to consider control of all data elements. Data entry and editing can often be dramatically simplified and made more accurate by permitting only correct types of data to be entered in the first place. For example, a date field can require a date-type format, and be limited to dates falling within a specified range. Other fields can be set to numeric values, and the number of characters may be limited.

It is important to examine carefully the requirements for each field, in comparison with the capabilities of the DBMS selected, in order to optimize this function.

Determine the types of queries anticipated. Any item of information on which queries will be made needs to be accessible, requiring that such items be defined as searchable fields. An obvious example is personal names: if names are input into a single field in forename-surname order, it will usually be impossible to do a name query on surname because search normally starts at the beginning of a field, not the middle. Many systems, however, permit truncation, meaning that names can be input in a single field, in surname-forename order, and searched only on surname.

In our publisher database, queries will be made for the sales history of recent publications of an author, or for the schedule for completion of a work in progress. In royalty negotiations, this and other information will be of value.

In our PDR database, all the existing index data will be queried, but it could also be desirable to build in other relationships—e.g., drugs related chemically or by application; interactions, etc.

In a newspaper database, it can be useful to query for particular types of item (e.g., illustrations, photos, syndicated columns, feature articles).

It is necessary to note that, while the conceptual organization of entities, relationships, and attributes described above is an important tool in database design, the actual implementation on a database package may not involve explicit definition of all these characteristics. For instance, relationships are usually not explicitly defined in the small DBMS we are considering, even though the designer must state them in order to assure that the necessary connections can be made for retrieval. Similarly, an "entity" and an "attribute" may not coincide one-for-one with a data element, record, etc.

Fidel (1987) and Soergel (1985) provide additional detail on database design.

Report Generation Using DBMS

Since database management software packages are generalized, and usually are not designed for complex text applications, their report generation facilities will not always precisely meet the needs of a given system. It is important to be aware of the capabilities of the software which is under consideration, in order to assure that satisfactory results can be achieved.

Sorting. The ease of sorting for output is a variable feature. Multi-field sorting (e.g., first on subject, then on author) is essential, and is usually available. The sort is normally straight character-by-character, including punctuation; it may or may not equate upper and lower case. This leads to orders which vary from the normal arrangements, and it may be necessary to shift records around later in word processing.

Squeezing superfluous blanks. If the software uses fixed instead of variable fields, the ability to squeeze blank spaces is required. In all cases, some fields may be blank, and it is necessary to be able to squeeze out these blanks as well.

Insertion of constant characters. The ability to insert constant characters (e.g., the period at the end of titles or "19" at the start of a date) permits both input savings and greater flexibility in output. Features designed to save time, however, may introduce complexity, as in the case of a title ending in a question mark; automatic insertion of the period would be redundant in this case.

Page formatting. Packages also vary in their ability to provide page-formatted output. The need for this sophistication varies, depending on the amount of manipulation in word processing that may be planned.

De-duping. Another important feature is the ability to match duplicates (e.g., subject headings) to avoid repetition in report generation.

Word wrap. The ability to run a field over to additional lines is not available in most DBMS, though it is possible to use the procedural languages in some of them to produce the equivalent.
For instance, in the PARADOX application described above, it was most useful to define the report for a subject index with each entry on a separate long line. This permitted word wrap to be

done in a word processing program. It also meant, however, that the page breaks generated by the DBMS had no meaning, because a single line output from the DBMS often became two or three lines in word processing.

Use of word processing. In order to achieve reasonable quality in output, it is generally necessary to do some post-processing in a word processing program. Most DBMS today can output to an ASCII file, and word processing software can accept such files as input.

While most word processing software can accept ASCII files, packages vary in their treatment of such files. The key is to get the software to look at the file as a document of its own, permitting it to be manipulated like any other document. Some systems are more helpful than others in this step. For instance, one system with which this author has worked accepts ASCII files and manipulates them like any other file with no difficulty, *except* that it ignores any boldface and underlining that may have been inserted, and ignores soft page breaks as well. It is really bewildering, because the file looks perfectly normal on the screen—the soft page breaks show up as expected, and so on. But all that comes out on printing is a long stream of undifferentiated text.

The documentation for the package provided no guidance on the issue. After much work, however, one day a new word processing document was defined and saved for the report heading information. Then the ASCII file was appended and the entire document re-saved. Suddenly, this document was a word processing document with all the expected page breaks and typographic niceties. If this seems confusing, that is probably only because it is confusing.

Once the data are in a normal word processing file, margins and indents are set and typographic refinements inserted. In addition, problems caused by use of labor-saving devices may need to be cleaned up. For instance, if a constant is used to insert a period immediately after the end of the title field, it is necessary to be sure either that variable-length fields are used or that the DBMS permits blanks to be squeezed, so that a result like this is not produced:

The Miller's Tale

If the period is inserted automatically, there will be duplicate punctuation for titles that end in a question mark or exclamation point. These must be deleted in word processing. This is generally very easy to do with a global search and replace command; however, there are pitfalls even here—the same word processing system mentioned above uses the question mark as its wild-card character. Thus, if one searches for the character sequence "?." and sets it to "?", one is actually searching for any character followed by a period, and replacing both the character and the period by a question mark. This means that the last character of every title (and every other string ending in a period) is dropped, and the period is changed to a question mark. Apparently, it never occurred to the designers of this system that anyone would ever want to search for the question mark itself. On the other hand, a search and replace on the string "!." readily produces the desired results.

Before acquiring a database management system, the indexer should carefully examine the interface with word processing, because the latter is the key to production of professional-looking reports.

By contrast, report generation with specialized indexing and bibliographic programs is relatively easy, but also more limited. Typically, indexing programs assume headings (to multiple levels), followed by locators that are page numbers. While the page numbers may be very complex, there is no provision for the locator to be something like a bibliographic citation. It may be possible to force such information to be treated correctly by the software; do a little investigation.

On the other hand, bibliographic programs expect something that looks like a bibliographic entry, and are not particularly hospitable to forms of information that cannot be expressed in this fashion. Most such programs permit post-processing with word processing software, but the need for these refinements is not as great.

Summary

An indexer faced with database design concepts may justifiably feel like the man who suddenly learned he had been speaking prose all his life. The indexes he or she has been producing are databases, but very limited ones. To write really good prose takes careful analysis and study as well as conscious effort. Database development places similar demands on the indexer, who needs to learn a variety of formal means of analyzing both a given set of data and the needs for access to it in order to utilize database capabilities effectively.

Use of database packages which are available today makes it possible for indexers to broaden their services and to produce more flexible products; however, to date the packages commercially available for PC's are not specifically designed for index-type applications, and indexers must learn to manipulate the available products to meet their needs. Once the indexer has done so, however, a whole new range of possible products becomes available. Many publishers have not yet learned how to make effective use of computers in actual development of their publications, and they welcome aid in doing so. Indexers' expertise in the organization of information is precisely what such publishers need. Mastery of database design concepts opens doors to more interesting work—and more of it—for the professional indexer.

References

Fidel, Raya. *Database Design for Information Retrieval: A Conceptual Approach*. New York: John Wiley; 1987.

Soergel, Dagobert. *Organizing Information: Principles of Data Base and Retrieval Systems*. Orlando, FL: Academic Press; 1985.

Indexing for Print, Online, and CD-ROM: Introduction to the Theme

The next topic on the program was suggested by the speaker. Barbara Preschel can speak authoritatively on almost every topic on the program, but she conveyed to me her interest in comparing indexing for print, online, and CD-ROM. In the syllabus for my indexing course at St. John's University, I include a question-and-answer column written by Mrs. Preschel a few years ago in the ASI Newsletter *(69, Nov-Dec 1984), in which she contrasts consultation of a book index with searching an online database; I consider this piece a classic. As Executive Director of PAIS, which has print, online, and CD-ROM versions, Mrs. Preschel will speak from first-hand knowledge on this topic. Those of you who went to the National Online Meeting exhibits during the past few days must have noticed that almost every bibliographic database is now available on CD-ROM, which indicates what a hot topic this is.*

Barbara Preschel *has a background as a librarian. She began working with computerized information storage and retrieval systems in 1961 as a bibliographer for the National Council on Crime and Delinquency. Mrs. Preschel taught for seven years at the Graduate School of Library and Information Science at CUNY-Queens College. She was Index Manager for the* Academic American Encyclopedia—*the first machine-readable encyclopedia (1980)—which had both a print and an electronic index, and was also the Index Manager of the* Funk and Wagnalls New Encyclopedia, *1983 ed. Barbara Preschel has been a free-lance indexer and a database designer, and is currently Executive Director of PAIS—Public Affairs Information Service, Inc. She is a past President and Board member of the American Society of Indexers.*

B. H. W.

Indexing for Print, Online,and CD-ROM

Barbara M. Preschel

Introduction

Indexing serves no purpose unless, at some point, the information that has been indexed and stored is used. Indexing serves no purpose unless there is also retrieval. Retrieval techniques have changed drastically since the advent of electronic indexes, and the techniques and capabilities of electronic retrieval of information have had an effect on indexing. There are differences between indexing for print indexes and indexing for electronic indexes that are caused by the differences in retrieval techniques. There also seems to be emerging a need for differences in indexing for retrieval from electronic indexes to online databases and electronic indexes to CD-ROM, which began to appear in 1985-86. This paper considers some of the ways in which print indexes to books and serials differ from electronic indexes to online databases and CD-ROMs. Full text searching, except as an adjunct to indexing, is not discussed.

Browsability

Because it is usual for more than one index heading and subheading to be displayed on a page in a print index, neighboring headings are serendipitously browsable, and an index user cannot help but view a number of index headings and subheadings at a time. This provides a contextual aspect to the user's search, that is often invaluable in suggesting additional appropriate headings or heading/subheading combinations. Of course, this is browsability within one part of an alphabetic array only, and the number of headings accessed is relatively small.

When an index heading, keyword, or descriptor is used to search an electronic index to an online database, the index does not automatically present the user with alphabetically neighboring headings with the serendipitous browsability of a print index. The user sees only the term that he or she has input on the screen, and if a specific word or words has been input, the user retrieves only material associated with that specific word or combination of words.

There are two ways to get serendipitous browsability in an electronic index to an online database. One is to view the thesaurus, if there is one online. Because the headings in the thesaurus must be viewed without the text of the data records to which they were assigned, this viewing gives the user less information than he or she gets when viewing the headings on the pages of a printed index.

The second way, and the way used most often to get serendipitous browsability in indexes to online electronic databases, is *truncation*. Most electronic indexes have command languages that allow for the truncation of terms. This gives a kind of serendipitous browsability in that when a word stem such as FAMIL is input followed by a symbol for truncation such as ?, it gives the user material indexed under terms like:

> Family
> Family—Economic aspects
> Family—Statistics
> Family—Tax aspects
> Family allowances
> Family corporations
> Family courts
> Family farms
> Family life
> Family planning
> Family size
> Family violence.

FAMIL? searches the neighboring terms in the alphabetic array beginning with that word stem in a way that mimics an alphabetic index print array.

This truncated search term in an electronic index will, however, also retrieve:

> Black families
> Farm families
> Single parent families

because the search is not limited to the left side of the term in the alphabetic array. Thus, a word stem in an electronic index will most likely retrieve more than a similar search in an alphabetically ordered print index with all its browsability.

Truncation often gives the searcher of an electronic database more retrieval than he or she intended to get. The searcher is often unaware of the vast number of terms that are being accessed in the search when a word stem is used. Far from being the relatively weak aid that serendipitous browsability is in a print index, the ability of an electronic index to retrieve materials that are associated with a particular word stem is like the power given to the sorcerer's apprentice. This is true for an electronic index to an online database and for an electronic index to CD-ROM.

Therefore, one of the problems in the retrieval of information from an online database using an electronic index is that the set retrieved may be too large. Searchers deal with this by narrowing the search: adding terms to the search statement or limiting retrieval by date, language, format, etc. They are often not decreasing the number of items retrieved on the basis of whether or not the items contain information of use to them. They are not reviewing the individual items. They are decreasing the number of items on the basis of the time needed to read the items once retrieved and the money needed to pay the database producer and database host for retrieval and printing or display of the items.

These same techniques for narrowing a search are used to arrive at reasonably sized sets of retrieved data records from CD-ROMs; however, they are not used in quite the same arbitrary manner. The advantage that the CD-ROM has over the online database, in this instance, is that although a large retrieved set will, of course, cost the searcher more in terms of time to look at the items retrieved, it will not cost him or her more in terms of money. The searcher is freer to pursue the elusive peripheral fact or idea, just as when using a print index.

Proximity to the Full Text That Was Indexed

If the print index is a back-of-the-book index, it is in proximity to the material indexed. This proximity means that the index user has additional data relatively handy for purposes of narrowing a search. It does not relieve the indexer of the responsibility for identifying and characterizing accurately the indexable information in the text. It does mean, however, that the index user has a relatively easy way to verify whether the indexer was using the heading in the same sense as the user, or whether another heading would be more appropriate.

In an electronic index to an online database or to a CD-ROM, it is rare for the full text of the original document indexed to be in close proximity to the index. A condensed document surrogate is usually the only text that is relatively proximate. This text may participate in the actual search process when an electronic index is used, and it is also often the text that is retrieved by the search process. It bears a heavy burden and must be constructed with multiple uses in mind. This is true for both an index to an online database and an index to a CD-ROM. The future of CD-ROM technology, however, will probably include discs on which both the index and the full text of the indexed materials reside. As in a back-of-the-book index, the capability will exist for the user to scan back and forth between the index and the full text. As in an electronic index, the user will have the full power of Boolean algebra, truncation, nesting, adjacency, etc.

Pre- and Post-Coordination of Terms

A heading/subheading combination in a print index pinpoints the exact aspect of a concept discussed in the text. The heading/subheading combination is bound together at the time the index is created, and represents subjects the indexer perceived in the text of the material being indexed. When the entry

> Probation officers
> Detroit

appears in the back-of-the-book index, it is because there is information on this topic in the book.

In an electronic index, headings are not bound together at the time the indexing is done. The relationships between or among terms are established by the user at the time that he or she is searching the database.

Even in the rare electronic database that has pre-coordinate terms just as print indexes do, in that multipart descriptors are contained in the controlled vocabulary, the searcher may choose to search on single words or word stems and ignore or override relationships established at the time of indexing in a way that users of a print index cannot. The fact that the user establishes the relationship between search terms at the moment that he or she is searching—and is not limited by the relationships that the indexer perceived in the text at the time of indexing—constitutes another capability that makes searching an electronic index a powerful method of information retrieval; however, because the searcher is concatenating terms in a search statement without knowledge of the concepts in the text, a search may not retrieve any documents at all. There may be zero hits. When the terms ''Probation officers'' and ''Detroit'' are concatenated in a search statement for an electronic index, the concatenation expresses the topic that the user *hopes* to find in the database, not necessarily a topic that *is* actually in the database. Pre-coordinate terms in a print index express the indexer's certainty; post-coordinate terms in an electronic index express the index user's hopes. This is true for electronic indexes to both online databases and to databases on CD-ROM.

Precision of Terms

A print back-of-the-book index is a finite thing. Once it is printed, neither the index nor the text will change. The indexer must be concerned only with indexing the text in hand. If the text is changed, there will be a new edition or a reprinting, and it may be assumed (or one hopes) that the index will be modified to reflect the actual text of the new edition. This is a closed-end index, and the terms should be as precise as possible, each term labeling the exact aspect of the topic covered in the text.

In indexes to serials, to collections of books and serials, and to online electronic databases, it is expected that the text to be indexed will increase as more items are included in the database, or new issues of the serial are published. Therefore, the index and the index headings must be planned to be added to, planned to be hospitable. This is an open-ended index. The index terms should be broader and less precise than in a back-of-the-book index so that they can accommodate the new ideas and concepts that will surely appear in the newly added texts.

Although it is true that hospitality of indexing terms should be a consideration for electronic indexes to CD-ROM when the data on the CD-ROM is expected to be added to, there are many CD-ROMs which are archival discs, to which no more data will be added. This situation presents a unique opportunity. If it were financially feasible, or if the material on the archival disc did not already have an index, it would be possible to construct an index with the precision and accuracy of a pre-coordinate back-of-the-book index and the power of an electronic index.

So far, most archival CD-ROMs and their indexes have been duplicates of existing online databases. Decisions were made to master a whole online database on CD-ROM, or to segment the database chronologically or by subject. The indexing that was originally designed for online retrieval was simply copied along with the data (usually with some enhancements). An archival CD-ROM to which no more information will be added is a finite entity, and the index to it could be a closed-end index, just like a back-of-the-book index, with all the precision and accuracy that that implies. Since it could be searched with the powerful functions of an electronic index, it would probably give a level of relevant retrieval greater than any we have known.

Depth and Specificity of Indexing

A print index is generally limited in size; a certain number of pages or columns is available for the index. In an electronic index, however, the number of terms that may be assigned to a given p:ece of text is relatively unlimited. This means that the depth of indexing and the specificity of index terms can be much greater in an electronic index than they can be in a print index. The indexer has the luxury of indexing peripheral matter, although judgment must be used as to what is peripheral but deserves an index heading, and what is not substantive and should not be indexed. There is a great temptation to over-index in such an environment.

In addition, the electronic index's ability to search natural language terms free text to the full extent of the machine-readable material means that even a concept that is not recognized as indexable at the moment of indexing may be retrieved because the word that labels the concept appears in the full text. The ability to retrieve every concept in a text whether or not it was perceived as indexable at the time the material was indexed has its price. False drops, noise, irrelevance, and retrieved sets of documents that are too large to deal with plague over-indexing and over-retrieval in electronic indexes to online databases and CD-ROMs.

Controlled Vocabulary Index Terms

Closed-end print indexes to books are usually natural language indexes in that the indexer may choose any heading that is suitable when a concept is first encountered in the text. The only constraints on the terminology are those of accuracy, precision, and grammatical consistency. Print and electronic indexes to open-ended serial and multiformat publications usually do not have the freedom that the concept "natural language index terms" implies. For consistency, to prevent scatter of information, and to avoid unintentional synonyms, a controlled vocabulary is often used in an open-ended index. This means that index terms may have been established before the new text to be indexed was seen, sometimes even before it was written. This can result in the use of partial synonyms or headings that are inappropriate in some ways to the material being indexed. Headings established in the past persist to haunt the pages of open-ended serial and multiformat indexes, both print and electronic, and headings that seemed acceptable once, may now indicate antiquated or awkward segmentation of a topic.

Antiquated or inappropriate index headings in electronic indexes to online databases are occasionally updated. Global changes may be made in which all term *X* headings are changed to term *Y*. This happens rarely, and is usually fraught with unforeseen problems. It is a massive and expensive job, which both online database producers and online database hosts are very reluctant to undertake. One of the major stumbling blocks is that it requires remounting the entire database and re-creating all of the inverted indexes. It may be possible in the future to replace antiquated or inappropriate headings in electronic indexes to CD-ROMs more easily than in online databases. Each time new information is mastered on a CD-ROM, all the data on the disc is remastered. Re-mastering the CD-ROM allows changes to be made in the data previously recorded.

Customization of Index Point of View

Usually a print index can be approached by the user in only one way. The index has been arranged according to one point of view. For instance, it may be approached by subject, by name, or by author, or it may be classified by historical period.

Electronic indexes usually allow for more than one type of approach. The electronic index can be searched by series title, by journal name, by date, by subject, by author, etc. If an approach from one point of view does not retrieve what is needed, it is customary for the online or CD-ROM user to try another.

The approach that the user must employ when consulting a print index is usually decided upon and fixed for all time by the indexer, often in consultation with the editor of the text, when the index is constructed. It is customized for the material being indexed. The approaches that the user can employ when consulting electronic indexes to online databases are often determined by the database producer in consultation with the organization that mounts the database, that is, the database host, distributor, or vendor. Typically, the database host is mounting more than one database and is using the same indexing and retrieval technologies for all. There is a Procrustean bed for which the database's toes or feet have to be chopped off or stretched out to make them fit.

One of the ways in which electronic indexes on CD-ROM differ from electronic indexes to online databases is that, since each disc is a finite entity, the indexing and the approach to the indexes can be tailored specifically for the material on the disc without consideration of the appropriateness of the index to other databases. This characteristic is shared by print indexes, particularly back-of-the-book indexes.

Conclusion

Although print indexes and electronic indexes to online databases share many characteristics, each has certain unique capabilities and felicities. As we gain more experience in creating electronic indexes for CD-ROM, we may find that they have some unique capabilities as well—some related to the capabilities of online indexes, others related to the capabilities of traditional print indexes. We may also have the opportunity of retrieving some of the capabilities and felicities of back-of-the-book indexes that we were forced to abandon when we fell in love with the capabilities, felicities, and power of electronic indexes to online databases.

Vocabulary Control: Introduction to the Theme

In a paper presented this morning, Hans Wellisch mentioned research on linguistics and indexing (which happens to be my major interest), and this theme is further developed in our next paper.

Both book and serial indexers must be concerned with the natural language problems of synonymy and ambiguity. Book indexers create an internal syndetic structure, whereas serial indexers generally consult thesauri.

Recently, the need for vocabulary control has come into question. One of the experts on this question is our next speaker. (I organized the program logically, but I cannot think of a better person to prevent post-prandial snoozing than Everett Brenner. He's a very exciting and entertaining speaker.)

Everett H. Brenner *has been manager of the American Petroleum Institute's Central Abstracting and Indexing Service for the past twenty-nine years, and will be retiring from that position in August of this year. For the next three years he intends to consult, teach, conduct seminars, and do some devil's advocate writing for information journals and newspapers. He has done some of that recently in an article in* Information Today *(April 1988).*

Mr. Brenner has taught information science courses at Pratt Institute, the City University of New York, and Columbia, and is chief designer and lecturer of the NFAIS [National Federal of Abstracting and Information Services] Seminar, "Indexing in Perspective." He is co-author, with Tefko Saracevic, of Indexing and Searching in Perspective, *published in 1985 by NFAIS. Last year he was honored by the National Federation of Abstracting and Information Services (which took Indexing out of its name) as the Miles Conrad Lecturer. His paper, "Information Retrieval—A 35 Year Personal Perspective," has been published in the Fall 1987 issue of* Science and Technology Libraries.

B. H. W.

Vocabulary Control

Everett H. Brenner

Historical Perspective

I discarded an unfinished first version of this paper because it was a rehash of what I and others had already written rather recently. My historical presentation on indexing, published by NFAIS in 1985, contains a major section on controlled and uncontrolled vocabularies. In 1986, Pablo Dubois of the International Coffee Organization in Britain presented a paper at a Cranfield seminar in England entitled, "Free Text vs. Controlled Vocabulary; A Reassessment." And, again in 1986, Elaine Svenonius (UCLA) published her paper "Unanswered Questions in the Design of Controlled Vocabularies" in the *Journal of the American Society for Information Science.*

I decided a rehash would not do for a sophisticated audience and an anniversary seminar at that. And, I recalled that when I had read the Svenonius paper, that her historical perspective on free-text versus controlled vocabulary presented a picture different from mine and decided that perhaps that difference needed exploring.

As an academician well-founded in library literature and history, Elaine Svenonius describes three eras. In the nineteenth century, she notes the increasing popularity of title-term indexing to aid the man on the street who could not cope with the classed catalog. She mentions Samson Low and Crestadoro as important figures of that time in favor of uncontrolled title-terms, and then Cutter, who gave us our system of alphabetical subject headings that dealt the death blow to title-term indexing.

Era two begins with the advent of the computer. Called the era of large retrieval experiments, it takes us up to the middle of the 1970s. This section of the paper mentions Hans Peter Luhn's KWIC (quick and dirty) index of 1959, and embarks on a discussion of mainly the Cranfield experiments, which compared large indexing systems using varying degrees of vocabulary control. According to the Svenonius paper then, this era is notable for introducing us to "the operational definitions of retrieval performance in terms of precision . . . and recall. . . ."

In era three, the 1970s and on, Svenonius describes many controlled vs. uncontrolled studies, out of which emerges one consistent finding, viz. that controlled and uncontrolled vocabularies have different properties and thus behave differently in retrieval.

The Svenonius paper then goes on to discuss in detail areas of research needed to improve the design of future retrieval tools, such as thesauri.

I and others arrived on the information scene in Svenonius' Era Two without library background, oriented to satisfying the information needs of research scientists in highly competitive industrial environments. In my historical perspective, I too describe three eras, the 1950s, the 1960s, and the 1970s. My first two eras, the '50s and '60s, fit nicely into the second of Svenonius' eras, but there are omissions and viewpoints in her paper that I think it most important to analyze.

In going back into the last century and describing how Cutter, exemplifying controlled vocabulary, defeated Low and Crestadoro, who advocated free text, the Svenonius paper seems to conclude that the future would inevitably be one with controlled vocabularies–hence, the title of her paper, "Unanswered Questions in the Design of Controlled Vocabularies." In the fifties, we looked to the computer to one day eliminate the need for controlled indexing, a costly and inadequate system for the strangling growth of the literature. Strangely missing from the Svenonius paper is the name of Mortimer Taube, who expounded the full text approach with his uniterms and concept coordination. To understand the Taube approach is to understand the advantages and disadvantages we face with controlled and uncontrolled vocabularies online today. Mortimer Taube's uniterms and concepts were quite different from Crestadoro's title words when you added the power of the computer. The alphabetical entries of a thesaurus were also meant to be quite different from Cutter's subject headings. The thesaurus as we know it was devised as an interim step to control free-text type natural language, because we had not yet been able to teach the computer to control it for us. Technology in the fifties had not caught up, but we hoped it would.

In that decade, the difference between precoordinate and postcoordinate systems became clear. Precoordinate vocabularies were controlled and not derived from full-text language; postcoordinate vocabularies, even controlled, such as in thesauri, contained terms derived from full-text language. Postcoordinate language had arrived on the scene because of the advent of the computer. Language that was manipulable by computer had advantages, and could affect the amount of control needed in any system.

Current Views on Vocabulary Control

In controlled vocabulary systems based upon natural language, the thesaurus is, at present, accepted as one of the strongest devices for imposing the control desired. Following the advent of uniterm systems that tried to free the vocabulary from all constraints and allow information to be identified and retrieved in the natural language of the document (i.e., the words used by the original author), the thesaurus emerged as a necessary tool. It provided a level of control on natural language through linkage of synonyms and near-synonyms and by identification of relationships among terms.

It is important to recognize, however, that a thesaurus is expensive to maintain. It must be continually responsive to changes in natural language, and interrelationships between words must be closely studied each time a change is made. When a thesaurus is revised, the tendency has been to revert to pre-coordinated entries; the thesaurus then ends up being very similar to a subject heading list. Failure to maintain the thesaurus adequately and failure to maintain its "keyword" (natural language) characteristics reduce its strength as a tool for post-coordinate computer manipulation of natural language.

We are now beginning to close out the decade of the '80s, and where are we concerning vocabulary control and full text? Elaine Svenonius tells us the one thing we've learned is that controlled and uncontrolled vocabularies have different properties and thus behave differently in retrieval. Pablo Dubois in his reassessment concludes as follows:

> What emerges most clearly from this review is that a partisan approach to free text and controlled vocabulary retrieval cannot be justified. It may well be unwise for retrieval technologies to minimize structures when dealing with a structured entity language. Retrieval performance is so affected by extraneous variables that optimal solutions are unlikely to be uniform, this does not therefore even imply that both approaches should be recommended concurrently. What is needed most, particularly in the context of new ways of formatting queries, is a clearer understanding of the operation of both the absolute and relative, of the various techniques in carefully described discrete environments, allowing a precise identification of the relevant variable.

Carol Tenopir, in her paper in *Library Journal*, in 1987 says that:

After examining the results of over 20 years of research studies and looking at search strategies from searchers of all levels of experience, the only answer I can give to the free-text vs. controlled vocabulary dilemma is it depends. It depends on: 1) the database; 2) the vocabulary itself and the indexing policies that dictate how it is applied; 3) the topic to be searched; and 4) the requester.

She goes on to summarize that "no one search method is the best in every database, for every topic, or for every requester. The ability to use a combination of controlled vocabulary and free-text techniques or change strategies online is the mark of good searchers."

In other words, there is literally a jungle of vocabulary systems and free-text out there. You must use not only all the systems and techniques to be successful, but you must also be skillful at it.

Let's pursue this further and describe the jungle in terms of my and Elaine Svenonius' historical perspectives. The controlled systems have failed to solve all retrieval problems. Traditional classification and subject heading systems were simply too discipline-oriented and restricting. Thesauri have also failed as natural language surrogates, mostly because thesaurus builders were not conscious of its dependence on computers nor of its purpose being that of an interim natural language surrogate. Varied and inappropriate traditional systems and well structured and poorly maintained thesauri are all a part of the database vendor market in which a searcher shops. On the uncontrolled side, full-text and natural language retrieval of bibliography, title words, and words from abstracts also fail because commercial systems do not have the sophisticated retrieval software to truly handle the kinds of problems controlled vocabulary systems have tried to solve. Truncation, neighboring and other such gimmicks do not an adequate natural language retrieval system make.

What the computer has given us in the '80s is the ability to interact quickly with a great deal of online text, controlled and uncontrolled. In fact, despite the inadequacies of controlled vocabularies and the software systems devised for uncontrolled text, we live in an era in which we have a multitude of text and indexes available for manipulation, thus a great many choices are available; and, an intermediary, truly skilled in specific database indexing systems, with the end-user/questioner at his side to interact and browse, can do a better search than at any time in history, given a comparable amount of information available.

The Future of Vocabulary Control

But what about the future? Given the fact that, in my opinion, controlled vocabularies have finally failed, and that indexing with and maintenance of even a good thesaurus are very expensive, should future research go in the direction of answering questions in order to design better controlled vocabularies as Svenonius suggests? I think not. Research is needed to discover how to better manipulate natural language from full text by computer in order to translate it intelligently into the language of users of an information system. Of course, all the work already done in defining controlled vocabularies will help in the research and development, but the approach must not be hindered by thinking that we will be developing indexing tools such as thesauri.

Unfortunately, because of the lack of research in artificial intelligence in our field at this time, nor any desire, it seems, to further develop automatic retrieval systems such as those based on Salton's relevance feedback approach, the 1990s may simply continue to stagnate in terms of breakthroughs in developing vastly improved controlled vocabularies or truly sophisticated software to tame uncontrolled vocabularies.

Some fairly recent expert system work is, however, worth noting as perhaps the new interim step in the next ten to fifteen years before we teach the computer to intelligently handle natural language. The American Petroleum Institute has developed an expert-based system which can translate the words of an abstract into controlled thesaurus terms, so that 70 percent of the terms posted for a document are selected by computer; the other 30 percent are provided by a human indexer. The significance of these statistics is that perhaps only 30 percent of our indexing actually involves intelligence, while the rest is rather simple-minded.

This system has the advantage of excellent indexing consistency and of lowering the cost of indexing (8000 documents are processed in this way per year), but it does not lower the cost of maintaining a quality thesaurus for an interdisciplinary collection or of developing and maintaining a specialized knowledge-based system of rules.

Moving in the same direction, but on the retrieval rather than the indexing side, Tome Associates Inc., based in England, has recently developed a retrieval system which can take the natural language of an end-user and translate it into a logical question which utilizes all the vocabulary available, including the controlled thesaurus terms of the database. This end-user approach is also expert-system based; development is very expensive. This development seems a logical one; given that we have both controlled and uncontrolled vocabulary available, the Tome Associates system attempts to utilize all that available information to help the end-user directly. It is noteworthy that the Tome Associates system is based on work done at the University of London by the Vickerys, pioneers in information science during the '50s. Another system with perhaps a similar approach in the U.S. has just come to my attention, that of Information Access Systems at Boulder, Colorado.

These expert systems are worthy steps to a future perhaps yet far away but inevitable, when an end-user can search a system driven by a computer which can read a question and search intelligently. Research in the coming years must not dwell on the design of a controlled vocabulary such as a thesaurus, but must concentrate on new ways or even further development of old ways to get the computer to translate, control, and/or manipulate natural text into the language of a query—in other words, controlling the uncontrolled, but in new ways. The words 'controlled' and 'uncontrolled' have negative implications—restricted and untamed, respectively. New systems will, we hope, merge the positive rather than the negative properties of controlled and uncontrolled language into tools that will aid all searchers.

References

Brenner, Everett H.; Saracevic, Tefko. *Indexing and Searching in Perspective*. Philadelphia, PA: National Federation of Abstracting and Information Services; 1985.

Dubois, C. P. R. Free Text vs. Controlled Vocabulary, A Reassessment. *Online Review* 11 (4): 243-253; 1987.

Svenonius, Elaine. Unanswered Questions in the Design of Controlled Vocabularies. *Journal of the American Society for Information Science* 37 (5): 331-40; 1986.

Tenopir, Carol. Searching by Controlled Vocabulary or Free Text? *Library Journal* November 15, 1987: 58-59.

Indexing and Classification: Introduction to the Theme

I can best introduce the next paper by sharing with you the correspondence between Jim Anderson and myself when I commissioned a paper from him on "Indexing and Classification."

Dear Bella, Thanks for your letter. I would be happy to prepare a paper for the May 13th ASI Annual Meeting, but I am confused by the scope of my assignment. If the overall theme is "Indexing: The State of Our Knowledge and the State of Our Ignorance," and I speak to "Indexing and Classification," what is left for the others?

This was my response: "Dear Jim, I know you think that indexing and classification are the same thing, but the scope of the paper I had in mind for you does not deal with the totality of index design, but instead focuses on the relationship between alphabetical indexing and hierarchical classification. What I would essentially like you to deal with is the complementarity of indexing and classification; to show that alphabetic indexes with syndetic structure in fact have hidden classifications. You might also discuss when a classified display of index entries is preferable to an alphabetic display and describe the generation of alphabetic index entries from feature headings of a classification. In sum, the topic I want you to treat is indexing AND classification in the Boolean sense, not the whole universe of indexing concepts, although you are undoubtedly qualified to do so."

Dr. James Anderson served on my doctoral dissertation committee, and it has been a pleasure to work with him and to exchange ideas with him throughout the years.

James D. Anderson *earned his B.A. at Harvard and his masters and doctoral degrees at Columbia University. He has taught at St. John's University and Queens College, CUNY, and now serves as Associate Dean and Professor at the School of Communication, Information and Library Studies, Rutgers University, in New Brunswick, New Jersey, where he specializes in database systems.*

He designed the Contextual Indexing and Faceted Taxonomic Access System (CIFT), now used by the Modern Language Association for its International Bibliography and Database on literature, language and folklore. During 1985-86, he designed a facet-based indexing and vocabulary management system for the J. Paul Getty Trust's Art History Information Program and the Centre de Documentation

Sciences Humaines in Paris. His students now design text-based databases using IOTA, software for "Information Organization based on Textual Analysis," which incorporates many features of the MLA and Getty/CDSH systems. IOTA supports vocabulary management, faceted and enumerative classification, and keyword, permuted, string, faceted, and precombined subject heading indexing. During the past year, it has been used by several non-indexer faculty to create back-of-the-book indexes using Timothy Craven's NEPHIS (Nested Phrase Indexing System).

A former chair of the American Society of Indexers' Education Committee, Dr. Anderson is also active in ASIS and has published extensively.

B. H. W.

Indexing and Classification: File Organization and Display for Information Retrieval

James D. Anderson

Indexing versus Classification

Last November, when Bella first wrote, she asked me to speak on "Indexing and Classification." I responded, "Yes, but if I speak on indexing and classification, what is left for the others?"

Bella responded, "I know you think that indexing and classification are the same thing, but . . ."

Well, Bella was right. I do think indexing and classification are the same fundamental operation, and, broadly conceived, they must encompass consideration of the following factors:

1. The scope, domain, clientele, and purpose of the collection or database to be analyzed and organized for retrieval;

2. Media, codes and symbol systems, including media used for compilation as well as media used for access and display;

3. Units of analysis, ranging from entire documents to individual statements;

4. Indexable matter—the raw material for indexing or classification;

5. Exhaustivity—the detail of indexing or classing; the number of terms extracted or assigned, or the number of classes in which an entity may be placed;

6. Indexing or classing method: machine algorithm or human analysis; entity-oriented or request-oriented; extraction or assignment; on the basis of symbols or concepts;

7. Indexing syntax (or class synthesis)—the combination of terms and classes;

8. Indexing terminology (or class size & relations)—issues such as specificity, equivalence, homography, hierarchy, and association;

9. Entity representation (or surrogation, to use one of my least favorite jargon words);

10. Record structure;

11. Record displays; and, last, but not by any means least,

12. File organization and display.

71

You are spared most of this, at least from me, but I lay it out here for context. No indexing or classification happens in a vacuum. Decisions are always made on all of these points, either consciously or by default, and each factor affects all others to varying degrees.

Bella commanded me to deal with "indexing AND classification in the Boolean sense," even though my Boolean sense tells me the original query ought to be indexing OR classification. Because fundamentally, indexing and classification are indeed the same operation. I'll tell you why this is so (at least in my opinion), then I will proceed to follow Bella's orders to the best of my ability.

Indexing is indicating features of entities or events using succinct descriptors, terms, headings, or indicators. Thus we have the Consumer Price Index, indicating the general rise and fall of consumer prices through the use of numerical indicators, and we have a wide range of text and document indexes using all sorts of alphanumeric terms and notation. *Classification* is the assignment of entities or events to classes on the basis of their features.

In indexing, each term names a group (a class!) of entities or events with which the term is associated. In classification, each class may be named by a term referring to the features that characterize the class.

Thus, indexing and classification have the same denotation; it's the connotations that differ. I accept the fact that to many people, classification *implies* the grouping of entities or events (or their representations) to a greater extent than does indexing. But good indexing also facilitates grouping—and, we hope, the identification of that special group of most relevant items.

The title proper of this paper, "Indexing and Classification," is followed by the obligatory colon and a subtitle with two aspects: "File Organization" and "File Display." The rest of my paper addresses these two aspects of indexing and classing. I begin with a discussion of the "Grouping of Entities or Events," looking first at the role of thesauri and generic posting, then at algorithmic grouping of entities on the basis of such attributes as descriptors, keywords, and reference citations. I then turn to file display, with examples from various types of indexing, including keyword, subject headings, string indexing, facet indexing, and enumerative classification, closing with examples of pernicious grouping.

Grouping Entities or Events

Thesauri and Generic Posting

In both indexing and classification, in Bella's sense, we create groups by means of vocabulary tracking and management (terms I prefer to 'control'). A thesaurus is the tool we use to gather concepts of importance in the domain of our index, and to match terms to these concepts. Once this is done, most thesauri endeavor to describe and display relations among concepts: genera and species, wholes and parts, disciplines and subfields, uses and agents [1], and a wide variety of less specific or less permanent associations [2]. It is these defined relationships that permit greater grouping, bringing together the species of a genus, the parts of a whole, the subfields of a discipline, and partners in other relationships.

A similar effect can be achieved—without the major investment entailed by a full-scale thesaurus—through what is often called "generic posting," the assignment of broad terms as well as specific narrower terms. While this can lead to helpful grouping for broad, *generic* searches, it can create havoc for *specific* broad searches when what is desired are entities related specifically to a broad concept, not to all of its species, parts, subfields, or associated aspects. (*Specific* does not mean narrow; it refers to closeness or goodness of fit.)

Grouping on the basis of thesauri or generic posting both imply a lot of human intellectual consideration of concepts and their relations. It is also possible to do a lot of very helpful grouping on the basis of entity attributes which may be manipulated by machine.

Entity attributes

Entities—documents, texts, or objects—may be grouped on the basis of terms they share in common. Such terms may be keywords found in titles, abstracts or full texts; assigned descriptors; bibliographic reference citations; names of authors, journals, publishers, or languages; dates; or any other named attribute.

Similarly, these terms themselves may be grouped on the basis of their co-occurrence in, or in relation to, entities. Grouped terms may then be used to locate additional, potentially relevant, entities.

Some examples:

Back in 1978, Tamas Doszkocs introduced a prototype term grouping mechanism called an "associative interactive dictionary." It ranked terms according to the relative frequency of their occurrence in a particular subset of documents as compared to an entire collection [3]. In his example from the TOXLINE database, a preliminary search was performed using the keywords PRENATAL and TOXICITY. The associative interactive dictionary then listed the following words, ranked according to their relatively more frequent occurrence in the retrieved set than in the collection as a whole: *prenatal* (I would hope so!), *postnatal, gestational, fetus, gestations, teratogenicity, embryocidal, perinatal, placental, mothers, clefts, retardation, fetuses, stillbirths,* . . . and on and on.

Most of these terms are clearly related—conceptually as well as statistically—and once identified, they can be used to broaden or narrow the group (or class!) of retrieved documents.

Conversely, documents—and by the way, documents can be texts of any size, from single statements to paragraphs, to pages, to groups of pages or articles, to books, to whole collections—documents may be grouped on the basis of shared terms. Of course, this is precisely what happens in the simplest of Boolean searches. Documents associated with the search terms are separated from all other documents. But more comprehensive clustering procedures may be applied to entire files in advance of searching in order to facilitate effective retrieval by focusing the search on subsets of potentially relevant documents. Gerard Salton's SMART system uses this approach [4].

Resulting clusters may be larger or smaller, depending on thresholds for intra-cluster document relationships and the extent to which clustered documents must share common terms or attributes. Salton has described typical class types as a "string," in which each document is related only to one other document—A is related only to B, B only to C, C only to D; a "star," in which all documents are related to a single core document; a "clique," in which all documents are related to each other; or a "clump," in which documents are not necessarily related to other documents, but to the group of documents treated as a whole [5].

Instead of terms or descriptors, bibliographic citations may serve as the basis for grouping. When documents are grouped on the basis of shared references, we call it "bibliographic coupling." When citations (representing cited documents) are grouped on the basis of co-occurrence, we call it "co-citation."

Similarly, any other document attribute may be used to group documents. Searchers often partition files, for example, on the basis of language, date of publication, document type, author, or journal.

File displays

Grouping can also facilitate retrieval through effective file displays. File display is crucial in print media databases—from back-of-the-book indexes to large encyclopedias, dictionaries, or abstracting and indexing services—since the way the file is arranged (or displayed) directly determines how both of the two fundamental search modes may proceed. These search modes are "lookup" or "select" on the one hand; "examine," "browse," or "scan" on the other. In electronic media, initial lookup is determined by internal file organization invisible to the searcher, but effective displays of parts of the file can facilitate effective browsing, scanning, or examination. Such displays are more essential as databases become directly available to less experienced searchers. Online public access catalogs are a prime example.

The degree to which entries may be grouped within a display is directly related to the extent and type of *syntax* that governs the order of terms within index entries.

For alphabetical indexes, grouping relies on consistent use of subheadings so that under a single lead term, entries are grouped by significant secondary aspect.

Relational indexes are frequently preferred for scanning larger groupings. (Many people call relational indexes "classified displays," but by now you know that all files and displays are "classified".) Relational grouping relies on the identification of facets. Entries are then arranged by facet, and within facet, by the terms representing the concepts belonging to a facet in hierarchical, chronological, alphabetical, or some other hopefully useful order. Thus, in literature, if you choose *nationality, genre, period,* and *author* as your "citation order of facets," then all entries will be grouped first by national literature, arranged possibly in a hierarchical order, so that all Romance literatures and all Germanic literatures are together. Since genre is the second facet to be cited, wit'7in each national literature, entries will be grouped by genre, which may be arranged at least in part alphabetically, since a hierarchy of genres is much less obvious. Within each genre, entries would be grouped by period, in chronological order, and within each period, authors would be listed alphabetically, since neither hierarchy nor chronology would make much sense for displaying the names of specific persons.

Now let us briefly survey different approaches to indexing and classification in terms of syntax, and therefore the kind of grouping they facilitate in file displays.

Keyword index displays

Simple keyword indexing permits limited grouping, because, by definition, no conceptual relations among terms are recognized.

KWIC (key-word-in-context) files are arranged under each keyword by whatever word happens to follow (or, in some cases, precede) the keyword in the indexing source—usually a title or title-like statement. Since that can't be predicted, there is no regularity or predictability in the resulting file. The entire subfile under a particular keyword must be examined. Thus, file display does not greatly facilitate examination or browsing.

KWOC (key-word-out-of-context) files are even worse because, under each keyword, they are arranged by the first word in the keyword source. At least in the KWIC file, you have the word following (or preceding) the keyword, so it is possible to see word pairs. Word pairs are dissolved in KWOC displays.

KWAC (key-word-alongside-of-context) files are designed to preserve word pairs, but to improve appearance by moving the keyword to the left margin. Subarrangement is based on the word or words following the keyword in the source statement or title, which is, in turn, followed by preceding words.

Permuted keyword indexes (for example, the Institute for Scientific Information's Permuterm Indexes) maximize the grouping of word pairs. The contextual benefits of multiple terms in natural word order is sacrificed in return for displaying all word pairs, regardless of whether they actually appear together in the source text. After stop words are eliminated, all paired words are arranged alphabetically, in turn, under each key word.

Subject heading displays

Subject headings are those venerable combinations of index terms whose syntax has grown up over time, indeed over the past century, since Charles Ammi Cutter propounded their virtues. I call their syntax "ad hoc," since it is very difficult to predict what kind of term will be attached to what, or how they will be combined, or in what order. Back-of-the-book indexes also usually feature "ad hoc" syntax, since, like subject headings, each individual heading is usually individually handcrafted to fit the particular occasion.

Nevertheless, some patterns have developed in subject headings (as they do also in back-of-the-book indexes) so that files generally facilitate examination and browsing once initial lookup is successfully negotiated. That initial lookup, however, has been seriously sabotaged in many library catalogs by the plundering of syndetic structure. The idea that the "normal" user will rush to a big red book (Library of Congress Subject Headings) [6] to find the equivalent and related terms that she or he should have been using—this widespread assumption has been proven, over and over again, to be far-fetched. Even librarians are loath to check. Syndetic structure—*see* references and *see also* references—were designed for integration into the catalog or index file. That is where they belong, and that is where they should be restored, especially in online catalogs and databases.

String Indexing

Since the introduction of computers into information processing, a new approach to index entry production and display has evolved with the inelegant name "string indexing." The basic approach involves the linking of terms that apply to a single text. Computer programs manipulate these linked terms, or "strings," to create individual index entries, and in turn, these may be grouped into files for display. Timothy Craven has described an enormous number of string systems in his book *String Indexing* [7].

The simplest approach to string indexing is exemplified by ABC-Clio's Spindex system. Under each lead term, other terms are simply arranged in alphabetical order, so that no particular relationship among terms is indicated by their sequence [8].

NEPHIS (Craven's Nested Phrase Indexing System) does not specify syntax, and therefore does not provide for any particular method for grouping entries in displays. Instead, it supplies a simple coding method, so that subject statements created by indexers may be transformed into multiple index entries by computer algorithm. At Rutgers, we have found NEPHIS to be an effective tool for amateur indexers (typically academic authors who have just written a book and want to index it quickly, simply, but effectively). They are fairly good at stating succinctly the principal theme of a textual element (usually a paragraph), but they have no experience or skill in transforming such statements into good, meaningful, sortable index entries. They can learn NEPHIS coding fairly quickly, however, and let the computer create the entries [9].

PRECIS (The Preserved Context Indexing System) bases its syntax on semantic roles, so that the place within a PRECIS string for a particular term depends on the role it plays in the overall subject statement. For example, does it indicate an environment; or an object of action; or an action or process itself; or an agent of action or related factor; or a part or property of some other entity or phenomenon [10]? The relations among terms are preserved in the individual index entries, giving a high degree of regularity in displays under lead terms.

Faceted indexing systems, such as the Modern Language Association's Contextual Indexing and Faceted Taxonomic Access System (CIFT) [11] or the Postulate-based Permuted Subject Indexing System (POPSI), developed in India [12], place terms in facets, and since facets are a fundamental building block of relational displays, faceted index strings may be used to create both alphabetical and relational (classified) displays. CIFT, for example, places terms relating to literature in facets for nationality or language, period, genre, authorship, work, style, theme, methodological approach, scholarly tool, etc. Each term may become a lead term in an alphabetical index, subarranged in a consistent and regular way by terms arranged in a consistent facet order.

Since terms are tied to facets, but the citation order of facets need not be fixed or specified in database records, an enormous number of relational displays, i.e., classified arrangements, may be created, on demand, from the same database records. In literature, for example, a relational display could group documents first by nationality, then by genre, period, authorship, and work; or first by theme, then by genre, nationality, and period; or first by methodological approach, then by genre, period, and nationality; or first by scholarly tool, then by methodological approach, nationality, period, and genre; etc., etc., etc. The possibilities are practically endless. Thus a "private" relational display can be created that matches the facet priorities of an individual client or client group.

Facet indexing also facilitates what Dagobert Soergel champions as "request-oriented" indexing [13]. He says, and I agree, that "A properly designed facet frame captures the essential conceptual structure of a field and is instrumental in eliciting the concepts to be included in the index language, in assisting in the analysis of a search topic, and in the analysis of an entity in indexing" [14]. A well-conceived facet frame for a particular discipline will represent the aspects of greatest interest to its members. For an indexer, it represents a kind of questionnaire to be applied to each document of interest. Does this document answer queries related to genres, methodological approaches, scholarly tools, themes, authorship, etc. The facet frame is a helpful guide to indexing, more explicitly helpful than the simple urge "to index whatever is important." Since such a facet frame provides a macro-view of a discipline, it can provide a framework for a thesaurus of its vocabulary, as well.

In a recent application of facet indexing for the J. Paul Getty Trust and the Centre de Documentation Sciences Humaines in Paris, a facet structure has been used as the basis for an expert system to create printed index entries. Indexing for two major Art History databases, the Repertoire Internationale de la Litterature de l'Art (RILA) and the Repertoire d'Art et D'Archeologie (RAA) (soon to be merged), tends to be rather exhaustive. The typical approach to entry creation in string indexing puts all terms assigned to a particular textual entity into each index entry. For RILA and RAA, however, the resulting entries would be much too long. They would violate Craven's criteria of succinctness [15]. Therefore, expert judgment was used to create frames of if-then conditions to specify what types of facet terms should appear in subheadings for each type of facet lead term. In other words, when an artist is in the lead position, what kind of information is most useful in subheadings? If an artist is in the lead AND a particular work of art is mentioned, what other facets are most useful? The same kinds of questions were asked for each facet and combination of facets— media, materials, iconographic genres and subjects, methodological approaches, etc., etc. [16]. The result is more succinct printed index entries without significant sacrifice of clarity and "eliminability" (the ability to determine irrelevance quickly)—two other of Craven's criteria.

In sum, faceted classifications are very flexible systems that facilitate the creation of alphabetical indexes with consistent ordering based on the order of facets.

Enumerative Classification

Enumerative classifications are lists of subject headings which are arranged in relational rather than alphabetical order. They tend to resemble traditional alphabetical lists of subject headings in that the particular headings represent combinations of concepts from different facets, and their combination and placement in relation to each other (their enumeration) has grown up over time. It is often difficult to see an underlying plan or philosophy. This is a principal difference between lists of enumerated classes and faceted classifications which are based on clear-cut facet order. In principle, enumerative classifications are applied in exactly the same way as lists of subject headings. It is only their arrangement that differs—relational rather than alphabetical, even if specific relations appear to be completely arbitrary or ad hoc. One of my favorite examples is the placement, in the Library of Congress Classification, of a class for socialism, communism and anarchism—including "scientific socialism," "left-wing socialism," and "bolshevism"—at the very end of the schedule for the social sciences, after social pathology and criminology [17].

Nevertheless, enumerative classifications can group entries fairly effectively. But all relational displays, especially when relations are "ad hoc" and unpredictable, need complementary alphabetical displays for initial lookup. No one wants to scan, browse, or examine an entire relational display, no matter how beautiful.

Pernicious Grouping

Grouping is not always good. Grouping can sometimes defeat retrieval. In print media, file display determines access, and therefore, structured displays based on esoteric principles that are hidden to even sophisticated searchers—to say nothing of the occasional or novice searcher—should be avoided. In the long, fascinating history of filing rules—which in fact deal with this very essential factor of file display and therefore, at least for print media, access to data—the public service camp of catalogers has succeeded in eliminating most remnants of secret structure [18]. The relative success of their long campaign is manifested in the 1980 *ALA Filing Rules* [19].

The Library of Congress, however, still clings to an ancient tradition that groups segments of its so-called alphabetical files in ways that stump even experienced librarians, to say nothing of filers. I have seen them stumble. The problem stems from basing arrangment on the type of entity represented in a heading or the form of name whenever multiple headings begin with the same word [20]. In other words, type of entity or form of name takes precedence over alphabetical order. Thus the tiny town of George, *Iowa* (population 1,241) is filed *after* Stefan George (i.e., George, *Stefan*), the poet, and both of these come *before* "George *and* Martha One Fine Day," the title of a book for children (grades K through 3). This order is decreed because when lead words are the same, headings representing persons are filed before headings representing places, which are filed before headings representing things (such as an airplane or boat named George), which are filed before titles. In a large file, 'George *and* Martha' could be drawers or pages away from where someone, simply relying on the alphabet, might expect to find this title. Similarly, in arrays of subject headings, the form of subdivision takes precedence over the alphabet, so that "Children—*Surgery*" comes before "Children,

Adopted'' and *''*Children, *Vagrant''* comes before *''*Children (*Roman* Law)'', all of which come before *''*Children *as* authors,'' to use LC's own examples [21].

Greater reliance on electronic files is diminishing this problem, but we still do, and probably always will, have extensive files in print media, so it's not too late to pay attention to searchers' knowledge and searchers' needs and eliminate secret obstacles to successful retrieval.

This example illustrates a basic truth. Structure can be very helpful when the structure is known and it conforms to the needs of a searcher. But structure can be positively disastrous when it is unknown. More than useless, it is a positive barrier to successful navigation through complex systems. The best structure is that which is optional, facilitative, and adaptive. Faceted indexes, for example, are highly structured, but this is facilitative, in that the structure may be used in many different ways.

Concluding Remarks

I hope it is now obvious to you, as it is to me, that indexing and classification are the same things, and what people mean when they make a distinction is really grouping and file display. Alternative ways to group related entries and creative ways to display files from lots of points of view, tailored to the needs and mind-sets of searchers, are concerns of increasing interest to scholars of human information-seeking behavior and information retrieval. They are very important topics about which we need to know a lot more. But, I am sorry to say, we don't even use now what we already know!

References

1. Soergel, Dagobert. *Organizing Information: Principles of Data Base and Retrieval Systems*. Orlando, FL: Academic Press; 1985: 282, 283.

2. Yih-Chen Wang, James Vandendorpe, and Martha Evens specify 43 different lexical and semantic relations. See their "Relational Thesauri in Information Retrieval." *Journal of the American Society for Information Science* 36(1): 15-27; January 1985.

3. Doszkocs, Tamas E. An Associative Interactive Dictionary (AID) for Online Bibliographic Searching. *Proceedings of the ASIS Annual Meeting* 15: 105-109; 1978.

4. Salton, Gerard; McGill, Michael J. *Introduction to Modern Information Retrieval*. New York: McGraw-Hill, 1983: 137-140.

5. Salton, Gerard. *Dynamic Information and Library Processing*. Englewood Cliffs, NJ: Prentice-Hall, 1975: 327.

6. Library of Congress. *Library of Congress Subject Headings*. 10th ed. Washington, DC: LC; 1986. 2 v.

7. Craven, Timothy C. *String Indexing*. Orlando, FL: Academic Press; 1986. xi, 246 p.

8. *ibid*, p. 26.

9. Anderson, James D.; Radford, Gary. "Back-of-the-Book Indexing with the Nested Phrase Indexing System (NEPHIS)," School of Communication, Information & Library Studies, Rutgers, The State University of New Jersey, New Brunswick, NJ 08903, March 1988. 21 p. Accepted for publication in *The Indexer*, Oct. 1988.

10. Austin, Derek; Dykstra, Mary. *PRECIS: A Manual of Concept Analysis and Subject Indexing*. 2d ed. London: The British Library, Bibliographic Services Division; 1984. xi, 397 p.

11. CIFT has been described in: Anderson, James D. Structure in Database Indexing. *The Indexer* 12(1): 3-13; April 1980. Anderson, James D. Contextual Indexing and Faceted Classification for Databases in the Humanities. *Proceedings of the American Society for Information Science Annual Meeting* 16: 194-201; 1979. Mutrux, Robin; Anderson, James D. Contextual Indexing and Faceted Taxonomic Access System. *Drexel Library Quarterly* 19(3): 91-109; Summer 1983.

12. Bhattacharyya, G. POPSI: Its Fundamentals and Procedure Based on a General Theory of Subject Indexing Languages. *Library Science with a Slant to Documentation* 16(1): 1-34; March 1979.

13. Soergel, 1985: 395-397.

14. *ibid*, 397.

15. Craven, 1986: 7.

16. The faceted indexing system designed for the new, merged RAA-RILA is described in: Anderson, James D. Knowledge Structure Representation: Planning & Design for a French-English Art History Database. *American Society for Information Science, Collected Papers and Abstracts, 15th Mid-Year Meeting*, fiche 1, paper 1, 9 p.

17. Library of Congress. *Library of Congress Classification. H. Social Sciences: Subclasses HM-HX, Sociology*. 4th ed. Washington, DC: LC; 1980. 169 p.

18. Anderson, James D. Catalog File Display: Principles and the New Filing Rules. *Cataloging & Classification Quarterly* 1(4): 3-23; 1982.

19. American Library Association. *ALA Filing Rules*. Filing Committee, Resources and Technical Services Division. Chicago: ALA; 1980. ix, 50 p.

20. Library of Congress. *Library of Congress Filing Rules*. Prepared by John C. Rather and Susan C. Biebel. Processing Services. Washington, DC: LC; 1980. vii, 111 p.

21. *Library of Congress Filing Rules*: 34.

Automatic Indexing: Introduction to the Theme

*Now we're going to tell you about the people who are trying to put you out of business—researchers in automatic indexing. I hope none of you brought rotten eggs or tomatoes, as I am also a member of that group, having done a dissertation on automatic indexing (*Word Frequency and Automatic Indexing, *Columbia University, 1981).*

At the 15th anniversary meeting of the American Society of Indexers, I presented the results of my research, demonstrating that index terms selected by humans do not match those selected by computer according to term frequency-based algorithms. What I remember from my dissertation defense is that Jim Anderson made me extract every statement that even implied *that human indexing was good indexing, or a standard against which automatic indexing could be compared.*

Today, automatic indexing uses techniques from the fields of computational linguistics and artificial intelligence. No one is more qualified to address the topic of automatic indexing than our invited speaker, Dr. Bruce Croft, who is a prominent researcher in this area.

W. Bruce Croft *received his Bachelors and Master of Science Degrees from Monash University in Melbourne, Australia, and his doctorate from the University of Cambridge (England) in 1979. Dr. Croft joined the Department of Computer and Information Science at the University of Massachusetts in 1979 and has been an Associate Professor since 1985. His research interests are in information retrieval, data models, knowledge representation, cooperative problem solving and user interfaces. The two main themes of his research are the design of techniques for representing and retrieving textual or multimedia objects such as journal articles, and the representation and support of complex, cooperative activities in organizations. He has published over 40 articles on these topics.*

Dr. Croft is an Associate Editor of the ACM [Association for Computing Machinery] Transactions on Office Information Systems *and of* Information Processing and Management. *He is currently chair of ACM SIGIR (Special Interest Group on Information Retrieval). He has served on numerous program committees and has been involved in the organization of workshops and conferences.*

B. H. W.

AUTOMATIC INDEXING

W. Bruce Croft*

Indexing and Retrieval

Unlike the previous speaker, I did not get a specification of what I had to talk about under the heading of automatic indexing, so I've been listening to the preceding talks with interest to find out what this audience means by indexing. The purpose of Figure 1 is to establish a common terminology between us. Why are we doing indexing? We are doing indexing—from my point of view—to do information retrieval (Belkin and Croft, 1987). That's fairly obvious. The usual case we are dealing with is that we have text documents, and have to represent the content of those documents in some way. Now in fact, that's a simplification of the world, in that the documents we usually have to represent are more complex than that, and can have multi-media content in terms of images, graphics, and very complex structure as well as layout. All of these things can be of interest for retrieval, as the previous speaker mentioned. In fact, there is research going on to represent the content of these more complex types of objects. For the purposes of this paper, however, I shall concentrate on the text content of documents.

The indexing process I'm interested in is to produce a representation of the content, the meaning of text documents. The reason we're doing that is not just for its own sake, but because people using our information retrieval systems have information problems—which are problems inside their head that we cannot get at. Unfortunately, we can't tap inside their brains yet. So what they have to do is—with the aid of a system, or humans interacting with a system—represent an information problem as some sort of query, using a language such as Boolean query, which is only one way of representing a statement, and a fairly artificial way. Perhaps one of the most reasonable ways of representing an information problem would be as a natural language description of that problem. No matter how the problem is represented, however, the next and most important component is the comparison of the query, which is a representation of the information problem, with the index, which is a representation of the content of the documents. We do

* Slide presentation by Bruce Croft. Text prepared for publication by Bella Hass Weinberg.

this comparison in order to identify relevant documents. Information retrieval is a *location* problem—a problem of locating interesting or relevant documents in a very large database of documents. That problem is different from other problems which natural language researchers look at, such as summarization or question-answering. Information retrieval focuses on the specific problem of locating interesting documents, and that's what we're trying to do with this comparison process.

In the field of information retrieval research, we are interested in three questions. First of all, how do we represent the content of text documents? Second, how do we represent the information problem that searchers have, and third, what is the appropriate way of comparing these representations in order to identify interesting documents—the documents which resolve, in some sense, the information problem. These are the topics of research that information scientists deal with.

It's impossible to separate the question of indexing from retrieval, i.e., the comparison part. You can't do indexing in isolation, which I've heard a number of people say already.

Human vs. Automatic Indexing, Figure 2, provides a categorization that I'd probably change after what I've heard various people say, but let me try and adapt it to what I've heard. The Figure provides a very simple classification of different approaches to this representation problem. At the top of the 2 x 2 table are the headings *manual* (or human) indexing versus *automatic* indexing, and the other two rows of this table are labeled *controlled* indexing and *free* indexing, or free text and controlled vocabulary, if you like. In one quadrant we have *manual* indexing—human indexing using controlled vocabulary. Current practice is to use human indexing plus free text—obviously there is not much indexing involved in using free text—you just use the free text at the searching stage.

The other two components are the ones of greatest interest. First of all, the lower right one, which is automatic indexing using free text, i.e., using the text of the documents. This is the best understood, and the one for which we have a number of experimental results, some of which have already been talked about today. I've labelled that quadrant *statistical information retrieval* because the models of retrieval (remember the retrieval and indexing process go hand and hand) on which these automatic indexing techniques are based are statistical models. They look at the meaning of texts by looking at the statistics of word occurrences in texts. This approach started with Luhn's work back in

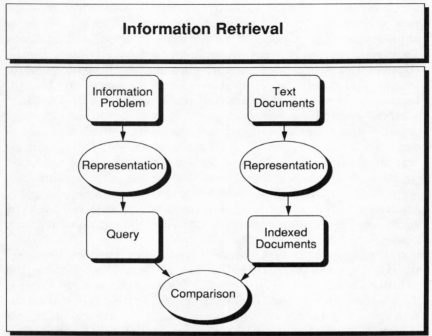

Figure 1

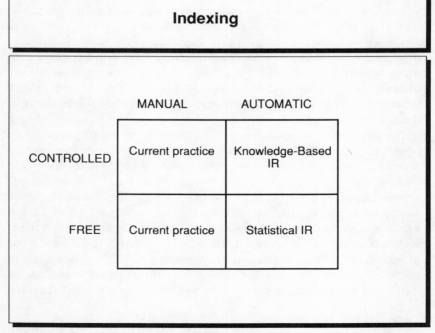

Figure 2

the '50s (Luhn, 1957) and has developed and come quite a long way (Salton and McGill, 1983). In the last quadrant, we have automatic indexing using controlled vocabularies. I did not distinguish between subject headings, subject indexes, and thesauri, but what I mean by controlled vocabulary is that there is some pre-specified vocabulary of concepts which describe a particular domain and relationships between those concepts. Now, if you want to argue how that's expressed—as subject headings or in thesaurus form—I don't really care. The key point is that there are pre-specified definitions of the interesting concepts in a domain and the relationships between those concepts.

This quadrant is called *knowledge-based information retrieval*, because in order to do natural language processing and more sophisticated forms of the comparison process mentioned above, you need some fairly detailed representation of a domain, and we can call that, if you like, a controlled vocabulary.

Simple Automatic Indexing

Figure 3 indicates what I mean by simple automatic indexing. This is the type of indexing that goes with statistical information retrieval techniques, which I won't go into the details of today, but most of you have probably at least come across or read some of Salton's books (e.g., Salton and McGill, 1983), so you have some idea of statistical information retrieval techniques.

A simple automatic indexing process, which we typically use in these information retrieval systems, involves first of all identifying a corpus of text, then removing the stop words (a list of about 300 very common words in English), stemming the words using a very simple algorithm for stripping out suffixes, replacing stems by numbers—just to make things a little bit more efficient from the storage point of view, and counting occurrences of those stems in a text. That's the statistical part—counting is statistics—so we just count how many times a word occurred in a particular text. Optionally, we use a synonym thesaurus to conflate the stems to represent by a particular number a group of stems relating to the same concept. I think you will agree that these steps are very simple, and certainly you can implement them in less than a page of any of your favorite [programming] languages.

The next steps are to calculate weights for the index terms that we picked out of the natural language, the weights that Salton calls *tf* by *idf* weights. These weights, as indicated in Figure 4, are a combination of the importance of a term as measured by the frequency of its occurrence in a particular document, and the

Simple Automatic Indexing

- Identify words in title and abstract of documents
- Remove "stop" words
- Stem words using simple algorithm
- Replace stems by index term numbers
- Count occurrences of stems
- (optional) Use synonym thesaurus to conflate stems

Figure 3

Other Indexing Steps

- Calculate tf.idf weights (within-document frequency plus inverse document frequency)
- Replace low "discrimination value" terms by thesaurus classes for low frequency terms, phrases for high-frequency terms

Documents before   Documents after
assignment of term   assignment

(Poor discriminator)

Figure 4

importance of a term as measured by its occurrence in a collection as a whole. These are various ways of getting these weights, but all the different ways are just variations on a theme; they are all measuring this basic combination of two things. Salton then goes o.1 to talk about *discrimination values* of index terms, vector space analogies of things moving in three-dimensional spaces.

The important thing is the *weighting* of the terms. Although this is often talked about as an automatic *indexing* method, the weighting comes from the *retrieval* model that this indexing is designed hand-in-hand with. Indexing isn't just done. You just don't put weights on terms because that's a good thing to do. The form of the weights comes from the particular retrieval model that you're using.

The experiments that have been done on automatic indexing have been designed to determine what are the most effective retrieval models, by measuring relative performance and by looking at theoretical performance as well.

The result that has been mentioned already today, and which is talked about a lot in Salton's papers, is that simple automatic indexing of free text in the form just described apparently works at about the same level of performance as manual or human indexing with controlled vocabulary. Now there are lots of qualifications you have to put on this statement when you look at individual experiments. The experimenters in this field have varied a lot in the way they have approached measuring recall and precision. I'm not particularly interested in arguing the fine details of this. Suffice it to say that there is certainly a lot of evidence to show that you can get very effective performance with these automatic techniques, and these automatic techniques are very cheap to implement. That's the advantage of simple automatic indexing: you can implement it very efficiently and very cheaply. You have to weigh the performance that you get versus the cost of implementing a technique.

Automatic indexing techniques are completely independent of the domain in which they are used. Whereas in manual indexing, you have to construct a vocabulary for a particular domain, with automatic indexing we are dealing just with the statistics of a text as controlled by the text itself. If a particular word is used often in a corpus, you'll find that out by counting it.

Figure 5 is from one of Salton's recent papers (1986) about recall-precision results from various experiments. As I've said, there are a lot of differences between these experiments, but it is very hard to explain away the findings of some of these experiments as methodological problems. There certainly seems to be a lot of evidence for the effectiveness of automatic techniques based on free text indexing.

But that's not the whole story. My recommendation doesn't finish there. I'm not saying that you should use only automatic indexing for information retrieval. All of the techniques represented in Figure 5 had fairly mediocre performance, and that's a common thing across most experimental results. We can talk about relative performance between techniques, but then when you look at absolute performance, you scratch your head and say—well, we're still doing pretty badly, even with the best technique that we've found.

So we're still missing something, and, of course, what we're interested in in research is: What are we missing? What is it that enables human beings to identify interesting documents so readily if they are shown a group of documents, and how can we get systems to perform more like that—to perform better than current systems? A number of results have been established that have already been mentioned. Automatic indexing of the type described, and manual or human indexing based on controlled vocabularies tend to have similar performance. It's difficult to say that one outperforms the other. When you look at the results of experiments, you note that although the methods have similar overall performance, they vary from one query to the next, and they usually retrieve different relevant documents. In fact, when you examine retrieval based on citations—which is another form of indexing—that also works quite well, and the overlap between the relevant documents this method finds and the relevant documents the other methods find tends to be fairly low.

Retrieval Models

This finding carries over to different search strategies. There are different retrieval models that researchers have investigated—the vector space model, probabilistic models, and cluster-based models. The first two are fairly similar from a theoretical point of view, but they both differ from the cluster-based model in terms of the underlying assumptions of how you represent content. The interesting results that we've gotten out of testing these models is that there is not a big difference between these strategies in relative performance, but they do tend to retrieve, once again, *different* relevant documents. They are looking at different evidence for relevance.

Manual versus Automatic

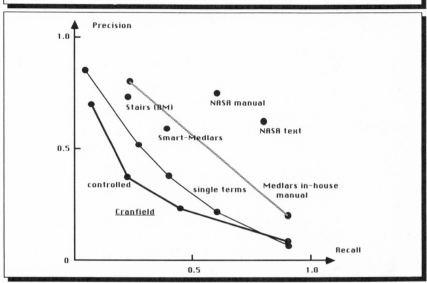

Figure 5

IR as Plausible Inference

- Retrieval is a process of finding plausible relationships between documents and the query
- There may be many such relationships betweena query and a particular document
- System's task is to quantify the overall plausibility or credibility of the relationship
- Inference can be viewed as

    Interested(Q) -> Interested(D)

- Inference is heavily dependent on request (user) model and domain knowledge

Figure 6

So what researchers are beginning to do is not try to identify what is the optimal representation for a document and the optimal search strategy to go with that representation to produce the optimal result. They're saying: Let's look at these things as alternative sources of evidence, which is essentially what is done in practice when free text indexing is used in association with controlled vocabulary.

What we're trying to do now is formalize this process of looking at different sources of evidence. We then have to have a way of combining these sources of evidence in a well-formed manner. In other words, we'd like to know what we're doing when we say we're going to use different sorts of representations in these different search strategies, which are going to give us different results. What we have to do is somehow combine those results.

The basic process of retrieval as we see it now in the systems we implement and in the formal models that we build is as follows. First of all, there is the process of building the request model, i.e., building the representation of the information problem. Some systems, such as *intelligent intermediary systems*, are designed to spend a lot of time building up that representation. Then there's the method of retrieving documents by a process called *plausible inference*, the details of which are given in Figure 6. It is a way of implementing the comparison process mentioned before, i.e., comparison of documents and queries. Then, there is also a *feedback* process of refining the initial request model by having the user evaluate documents that are retrieved, pointing out interesting components of those documents and using those indications to readjust the initial request model.

In research, we are starting to formalize this process of plausible inference. Another way of saying it is: formalize the process of looking at multiple sources of evidence and combining evidence in a well-formed manner to come up with an overall assessment for the relevance of a document. In other words, the relevance of a document is best assessed by looking at evidence from all available sources. If you have manual/controlled vocabulary indexing, for example, you don't ignore it, you use it; if you have free text indexing, you use that as well; if you have citation indexing, you use that in addition. Natural language processing techniques provide a different sort of evidence from the statistical techniques mentioned.

I am not going into the details of these models more than that, apart from saying that it's something that has been done for awhile in online searching, i.e., the use of free text as well as subject headings. This is a simple version of what we're trying to do formally and automatically now, i.e., to use all available forms of indexing and the associated retrieval strategies in order to assess the overall relevance of documents.

Domain Knowledge Bases

One of the experimental systems that we've built, called I^3R, is illustrated in Figure 7. It implements the preceding concept in the sense that its representation, or knowledge base (if you want to call it that—it's a very simple knowledge base), has documents, which are represented by some of the square nodes, with the dark shading representing terms derived by automatic indexing of free text. There are links (arrows) from documents to terms, and there are also concepts, which come from a controlled vocabulary. We prefer to call it a *domain knowledge base*, but it doesn't really matter what you call it. So we have both the automatically derived terms and subject headings in there, and there are relationships between them. There is also *nearest neighbor*, the *nn* relationships between documents and terms, which are automatically derived relationships, statistical relationships indicating similar content.

So what does all this mean—all these nodes and links? What it means is that given this representation, you can devise search strategies which make use of all these links as forms of evidence. There is citation evidence in there; there is subject heading evidence; there's free text evidence, and there are other forms of evidence as well—the nearest neighbor one, for example. What we've done is to devise search strategies that use all these forms of evidence. In fact, our initial results indicate that by automatically doing all of this—the user is not involved at all in selecting which search strategies to use—we get significantly better performance than any of the other strategies that have been tested so far.

The system just described is a simple one; as an experimental system, it is probably one of the most advanced systems implemented currently. But where we're heading is knowledge-based information retrieval (see Figure 8), and what I mean by that is the following: that our representations of the query and the documents are structures built by natural language processing, as one of the earlier speakers indicated. We are currently doing experiments with this.

Natural language processing technology is getting to the stage that we can build representations of context that are much more complex than, and have a much better representation of meaning

I³R Knowledge Base

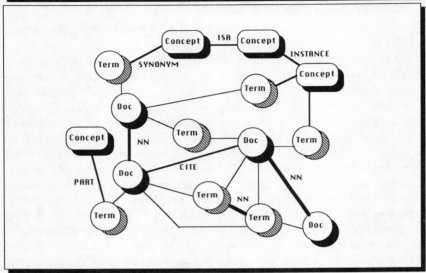

Figure 7

Knowledge-Based IR

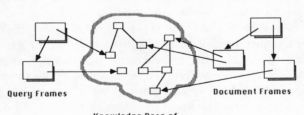

Query Frames   Document Frames

Knowledge Base of
Frames and Domain Concepts

- Plausible inference on knowledge base combined with frame matching on query and document representations
- NLP used to produce representations
- User models

Figure 8

than, either subject headings or simple automatic indexing methods. These representations tend to be structures built out of *case
frames*, if you happen to know that terminology, but essentially
what they are is relationships between domain objects. Where do
we get these domain objects, and how do we know which
relationships to represent? We have a knowledge base that tells us
what the important domain concepts are, what the relationships
between them are, and also what are the appropriate ways of
relating them as you would describe that relationship in text—in a
natural language query, for example. So what we end up with is a
representation of a query and a representation of documents
pointing into the knowledge base, because that's where the domain
concepts were described initially. A search in this type of environment involves both comparing the query representation and the
document representation, and looking in the knowledge base to see
which things are related to which other things. (Both the comparison stage and the representation stage get more complicated.)

Thus the broader-narrower term-type relationships that you have
used for a long time in controlled vocabularies become part of the
search process, and, in fact, that's what retrieval models tell us—
that we should view these things as part of the search process. Part
of this process of reasoning is posing the question: If a given
concept is represented in a query, what other concepts may be
related to that concept?

Getting back to the point I want to make about thesauri and
knowledge bases (and by thesauri I mean controlled vocabularies of
any type), I think that controlled vocabularies represent domain
knowledge (see Figure 9). You're trying to capture the important
concepts and the relationships between them. To do the sort of
knowledge-based information retrieval just described, we have to
have a knowledge base of that type. We have to know something
about the domain that we're doing retrieval in. We have to know
something about the objects in the domain and the relationships
between them. We also have to have linguistic knowledge. We
have to be able to relate those objects to ways we talk about those
objects in text in order to do natural language processing. The
important point is that you cannot do knowledge-based information retrieval without a knowledge base of domain concepts and
linguistic knowledge.

Thus, all the research about controlled vocabulary versus free
text is coming back to haunt artificial intelligence (AI) people,
although a lot of them don't know it. One point of disgreement I
had with the previous speaker relates to his statement that artificial

Thesauri and Knowledge Bases

- Thesauri and knowledge bases represent domain knowledge
- Automatic construction of thesauri/knowledge bases is hard (impossible?)
- Automatic, controlled indexing using knowledge bases may be more effective because

   a. More consistent than human indexers

   b. More detailed representation of knowledge

   c. Designed with search process in mind

Figure 9

Summary

- Automatic, free text indexing is cheap and effective
- Manual indexing can be used in combination with automatic indexing
- Future systems will emphasize knowledge bases
- Knowledge bases have to be built

Figure 10

intelligence researchers are not doing work on information retrieval. In fact, knowledge-based information retrieval is undergoing an explosion at the moment. A lot of people doing natural language processing work in AI have started to realize that information retrieval is a very nice application area for them to work in, and we're starting to see a lot more research in the area of knowledge-based information retrieval. Very few of us, however know anything about what has gone on before in information retrieval.

What I'm trying to point out is that it may be possible to use current AI techniques to do knowledge-based information retrieval at a certain level, but it appears impossible to build thesauri and knowledge bases automatically. In other words, generating a knowledge base from texts automatically—that is an extremely difficult task. People are looking at this problem, but they haven't gotten very far. You can produce a concordance of terms and things like that automatically, but that's only a very crude version of what I'd call a knowledge base.

So we return to the point that somebody has to build these knowledge bases, which means that somebody has to build a controlled vocabulary. Then you get into the question of: Well, what about the *consistency* between different people's views of the area? What if you represent it this way, and then a user comes up and has a completely different view of how a field is represented? I think it's interesting to see all these problems coming around again.

Summary

The key points of this paper are summarized in Figure 10. In answer to what Bella said—some of the things that you [indexers] do, I think we could automate tomorrow effectively. A lot of the other things that you do, we won't be able to automate for a long, long time. Yet other things that you do I think will change names and be incorporated into what's called knowledge-based information retrieval, because when you move into a new domain, somebody has to tell you what that domain's about—for the time being anyway.

References

Belkin, Nicholas J.; Croft, W. Bruce. Retrieval techniques. *Annual Review of Information Science and Technology* 22: 109-145; 1987.

Luhn, H. P. A Statistical Approach to Mechanized Encoding and Searching of Literary Information. *IBM Journal of Research and Development* 1(4): 309-17; October 1957.

Salton, Gerard. Another Look at Automatic Text Retrieval Systems. *Communications of the ACM* 29(7): 648-656; July 1986.

Salton, Gerard; McGill, Michael. *Introduction to Modern Information Retrieval*. New York: McGraw Hill; 1983.

Indexing, Searching, and Relevance: Introduction to the Theme

Up to this point, we have looked at indexes largely from the point of view of their creators, *humans or machines. Our next paper focuses on the intermediary searching our indexes, as well as the relevance judgments of the ultimate consumers or end-users of the information retrieved. The invited speaker, Dr. Tefko Saracevic, is the author of the classic paper on relevance, which he once told me was translated into seventeen languages. He also recently completed a major study on searchers that was published in the latest issues of JASIS. I consider him one of the greatest living information scientists, and we are honored to have the participation of Prof. Saracevic in this conference.*

Tefko Saracevic *studied electrical engineering at the University of Zagreb, Yugoslavia, and received an M.S. degree in Library Science from the School of Library Science, Western Reserve University in 1962. He received a Ph.D. in Library and Information Science from Case Western Reserve University, 1970. From 1962 to 1985, he held various teaching and research positions at the Matthew A. Baxter School of Information and Library Science, Case Western Reserve University. Since 1985 he holds a position as senior professor at Rutgers University, with primary involvement in the Ph.D. program and in research.*

Dr. Saracevic has participated as principal investigator or manager in a number of funded research projects. He is active in the American Society for Information Science (ASIS) in which he has held a number of offices. In 1985, he was the recipient of the ASIS Outstanding Information Science Teacher Award.

Prof. Saracevic has published articles in: Journal of the American Society for Information Science, Information Processing and Management, Journal of Documentation, Library Journal, Journal of Library Education, *and others. He has also published a book,* Introduction to Information Science, *and a UNESCO monograph,* Consolidation of Information. *A member of the editorial board of a number of journals and publishing series, since 1985 he serves as Editor-in-Chief of* Information Processing and Management.

B. H. W.

Indexing, Searching, and Relevance

Tefko Saracevic

Introduction

Indexes are created to be searched. No matter what type of index—whether created by humans or by machines—its major function is to be a searching tool. Searchers are the counterparts of indexers; however, searching as a process is different in many ways from indexing. Usually, searchers and indexers don't talk to each other and know relatively little of each other's work, accomplishments, and theoretical and practical problems. People who do research on searching rarely, if ever, cite literature on indexing research and vice versa. Yet there is an obvious connection, and perhaps more bridges need to be built between the research and practice of indexing and that of searching.

This paper summarizes some of the interesting results of a large study on information seeking and retrieving [1-4] that are relevant to comparison with indexing studies. The major emphasis here is to provide some insight on how searchers perform and how user context and type of questions affect the outcome of searches. The study was about people—users and searchers—and about processes—question-asking and searching, as opposed to studies of systems and databases; the difference is the same as between a study of indexers and indexing as opposed to studies of different indexing systems, schemes or algorithms.

This paper in itself does not build a bridge between indexing and searching studies. Its objective, however, is to provide some food for thought needed for such bridge building.

Description of the Study

The aim of the study (part of a long-term research effort) was to contribute to the formal, scientific characterization of the elements involved in information-seeking and retrieving, particularly in relation to the cognitive context and human decisions and interactions involved. The objectives were to conduct a series of observations and experiments—under conditions as close to real-life as possible—related to users, questions, searchers, and searching in information-seeking and online searching.

A group of 40 users was assembled, each posing one research question. A group of 36 "outside" professional searchers was recruited for searching these questions. Each question was searched by five different searchers. In addition, three project searchers performed four different types of searches, for a total of nine searches per question or 360 searches for the 40 questions. Users indicated, on various measures, the characteristics of the context. Searchers were tested on four cognitive tests. Questions were classified according to their characteristics in separate experiments. Searching was done on DIALOG; for each question, a single most appropriate DIALOG subject file was used (this is where we departed from real life); altogether, 21 DIALOG files were used. A union of output (full records from the DIALOG files) from the nine searches for each question was created and sent to the user for evaluation. The users judged whether each answer was relevant and indicated the utility of answers on five different measures. The results were expressed in a number of ways, most notably relevance odds and precision and recall. Of particular interest was the analysis of odds that a retrieved answer would be relevant as opposed to not relevant (in user judgment) based on correlations with variables associated with users, questions, searchers, and searches. This was a new method of analysis.

Counting the output, search by search, without elimination of duplicates, the 360 searches retrieved 8,956 items, of which 5,287 were judged relevant (or partially relevant), and 3,699 were judged not relevant by users. Counting the output question by question, with elimination of duplicates, the number of unique retrieved items was 5,411, of which 2,791 were judged relevant (or partially relevant), and 2,620 not relevant.

Measures

Four main measures were used to analyze the results: *precision, recall*, a logarithmic *cross product ratio* (xpr), and *overlap*. The first two are familiar measures in information retrieval: *precision* indicates the fraction of relevant or partially relevant items as judged by a user in a set of retrieved items, and *recall* indicates the fraction of relevant items in a search in relation to all relevant items in the union of all search outputs for a question submitted to a user.

The logarithmic *cross product ratio* (xpr) is a measure often used in biomedicine to indicate, for instance, the odds of smokers (one group or method) vs. nonsmokers (another group) to get a lung disease (one condition or result) vs. not getting lung disease (another result). We calculated relevance odds for *items* retrieved due to selected independent variables (for example, the odds that retrieved items would be relevant in searches with a high number of search terms), and we calculated precision and recall odds for *searches* (for example, the odds for high precision in searches with a high number of search terms).

Overlap measures indicate the degree of agreement between two searches with respect to search terms used or in items retrieved. The measure is asymmetric, indicating that agreement, when comparing search 1 to search 2, may differ from the comparison of search 2 to search 1. The agreement between search 1 and search 2 is calculated as the number of search terms (or items retrieved) shared in common, over the total number of search terms (or items retrieved) in search 1. The agreement in search terms between search 2 and search 1, conversely, is the ratio of terms in common over all the terms selected by search 2. Similar measures were used in studies of indexing consistency conducted two decades ago.

Overlap Results

Two aspects were studied for searches of the same written question: the degree of agreement in (i) selection of search terms, and (ii) total relevant items retrieved. Overlap was computed for each pair of searchers and their searches for a given question. There were 40 questions and five "outside" searches per question (done by professional searchers hired for the occasion, as opposed to "project" searches done by staff); for each search there were four comparisons (since a search was not compared with itself); thus there were 20 pairs of comparisons for each question. For 40 questions there were 800 (40 x 20) pairs of comparisons altogether, with results based on 800 overlap measures.

The mean overlap in assignment of *search terms* was 27% with a standard deviation of 20%. The distribution was not normal—the results are skewed toward the low end. For instance, in 20% of the cases, the overlap was between 0% and 10%, and in 44% of the cases, it was between 0% and 20%.

The mean overlap for all items *retrieved* (including relevant, partially relevant and not relevant items) was only 17% (with a standard deviation of 28%). For relevant or partially relevant only, it was 18% (with a standard deviation of 30%). The results were even more skewed toward the low end: in 58.6% of the cases for all retrieved items, and 58.9% of the cases for relevant or partially relevant items, the overlap was between 0% and 5%.

In general, the overlap in selection of search terms by different searchers who are searching the same questions is relatively low. Given the same question, different searchers tend to select a few terms that are the same, and a considerable number that are different. The overlap of retrieved items (whether all items or only relevant or partially relevant items) is also relatively low. In fact, it is significantly lower than the overlap in selection of search terms by the same searchers. It seems that, for the same question, different searchers more or less look for and retrieve a different portion of the file. They seem to see different things in a question and/or interpret them in a different way, extract different linguistic expressions and, as a result, retrieve different items.

Surprisingly, the search term overlap does not explain the retrieved items overlap. A regression analysis showed that only 2.5% of variation in overlap of retrieved items can be attributed to the overlap in search terms. In general, in searches for the same question by different searchers, the overlap in search terms and the overlap in items retrieved are not closely related.

Multiple Retrievals

As mentioned previously, each question was searched by five "outside" searchers; some answers were retrieved only by a single search, some by two searches and some by three, four, or five searches. Thus, some answers were retrieved multiple times, others only once. In fact, about 79% of all items retrieved (including relevant, partially relevant, and not relevant items) and 72% of relevant or partially relevant items were retrieved only once; 13% of all retrieved items and 17% of relevant or partially relevant items were retrieved twice; 6% of all items and 8% of relevant or partially relevant items were retrieved three times; and only 2% of all items and 3% of relevant or partially relevant items were retrieved four or five times.

The picture changes when we consider "not relevant" items: 86% were retrieved once, 10% twice, 3% three times, and 1% four or five times.

This brought us to ask the question: What are the odds that an item retrieved "n" times (that is, once, twice . . . any number of times from 1 to 5) for the same question by different searches would be relevant? In other words, we are considering here relevance odds of single versus multiple retrievals. The odds of an item being relevant or partially relevant as against not relevant for any number of retrievals (in this case, from 1 to 5) were about even—1:1 or 10:10. For items retrieved only once, odds dropped slightly to about 9:10; for those retrieved twice, they rose to 18 to 10; for those retrieved three times, they improved to 27 to 10; and for those retrieved four or five times, the relevance odds jumped to 33:10. They tripled! The more often an item was retrieved, the more the odds shifted in favor of relevance.

In general, the overlap in retrieved items for different searches for the same question done by different searchers is relatively low. The chances for relevance improved dramatically, however, for items retrieved by more than one searcher. To underscore the point, the more often an item was retrieved by different searches for the same question, the more likely it was to be relevant.

Related Studies

A number of overlap, or degree of agreement, studies of a variety of processes associated with representing, seeking, and retrieving information have been reported in the literature. Such studies address overlap either in human decisions (e.g., consistency in indexing) or in systems performance (e.g., retrieval from different representations) [5]. These studies are related to a large family of investigations in psychology and cognitive science on human variability in forming associations and concepts, and in naming. At their basic level, all such studies investigate differences in patterns formed by human minds. Since a majority of overlap studies of information representation, information seeking, and information retrieval have reported results in an equivalent range, a generalization may be in order.

Our results show that the overlap in selection of search terms by searchers is in the same range, if not somewhat lower, as the overlap in selection of index terms by indexers, found in many inter-indexer consistency studies done during the 1960s and early 1970s [6]. Interestingly, they correspond also with overlap results based on Dewey Decimal Classification assignments in online catalog retrieval reported by Markey and Demeyer [7], and with overlap and searching behavior in a card catalog compared to an online public access catalog, by Dalrymple [8].

The overlap in retrieval of items by different searches for the same question, as found here, is comparable to findings in various recent studies that observed overlap in retrieval between: different document representations, by Katzer et al. [9]; keyword index terms, or descriptors and citations, by Pao [10], Pao and Fu [11], and Pao and Worthen [12]; document sets clustered by co-citation and Medical Subject Headings (MeSH), by Rapp [13]; and descriptors and citations, by McCain [14].

Conclusions

A general conclusion may be stated: the degree of agreement or overlap in human decisions related to representing, searching, and retrieving information is relatively low. The agreement hardly reaches about one-fourth or one-third of the cases involved. The notion of "low" here may not, however, be appropriate. We do not know what is "high," and the observed ranges may be all that can be expected; they may be "normal." But however these findings on the range of human information behavior in these processes may be labeled, the results have a potential for a large impact on the direction of and choices in research, design and practice.

Of course, all this calls for explanation and further research. A number of studies in cognitive science and artificial intelligence have been devoted to learning something about how human intelligence finds (or imposes) clusters and concepts on a set of patterns. Some ingenious ways of studying this are reported by Stepp and Michalski [15]. We may interpret our overlap results in terms of an opposite concept, namely in terms of "de-clustering." A structure (in our case, a question) is decomposed or de-clustered by different searchers into a set of alternative forms (in our case, searches). While the files which are searched are structured, indexed and organized in ways that aim toward a clustering of answers, searchers seem to be working in a way that de-clusters them. This is an intriguing hypothesis, and we are following it in our next phase of investigation.

As noted by many critics, the present design of online subject access, be it through library catalogs or online retrieval systems, does not accommodate human variability in searching (or indexing). This calls for radically different design principles and implementations in order to accommodate the observed patterns, interactions, and differences in human information behavior, of which the overlap findings are one of the important manifestations.

Let us end the discussion of overlap findings with some practical implications. Searchers may be as consistent (or rather inconsistent) as indexers. Nevertheless, although searchers disagree substantially in the items they retrieve in searching the same question, when they do agree, they are likely to be producing relevant items. This suggests further that one possible super-strategy for the conduct of an online search is to have several searchers search a question independently, and then examine first the intersection (or overlap) of their retrieved sets. The odds for finding relevant items in such an intersection are dramatically higher than in individual searches as a whole.

This paper has dealt neither with an indexing method nor with an information retrieval technique, but rather with an often forgotten element of the indexing and searching cycle — people.

References

1. Saracevic, T.; Kantor, P.; Chamis, A. Y.; Trivison, D. A Study of Information Seeking and Retrieving. I. Background and Methodology. *Journal of the American Society for Information Science.* 39(3): 161-176; 1988.

2. Saracevic, T.; Kantor, P. A Study of Information Seeking and Retrieving. II. Users, Questions and Effectiveness," *Journal of the American Society for Information Science.* 39(3): 177-196; 1988.

3. Saracevic, T.; Kantor, P. A Study of Information Seeking and Retrieving. III. Searchers, Searches, and Overlap. *Journal of the American Society for Information Science.* 39(3): 197-216; 1988.

4. Saracevic, T.; Kantor, P.; Chamis, A. Y.; Trivison, D. *Experiments on the Cognitive Aspects of Information Seeking and Retrieving. Final Report for National Science Foundation Grant IST-8505411.* Springfield, VA: National Technical Information Service; (PB87-157699/AS). Bethesda, MD: Education Research Information Center; 1987. (ED 281530).

5. Belkin, N.; Vickery, A. *Interaction in Information Systems: A Review of Research from Document Retrieval to Knowledge-Based Systems.* London: The British Library; 1985. (Library and Information Research Report, 35).

6. Zunde, P.; Dexter, M. E. Indexing Consistency and Quality. *American Documentation.* 20(5): 259-267; 1969.

7. Markey, K.; Demeyer, A. N. *Dewey Decimal Classification Online Project: Evaluation of a Library Schedule and Index Integrated into the Subject Searching Capabilities of an Online Catalog.* Dublin, OH: Online Computer Library Center (OCLC); 1986.

8. Dalrymple, P. W. *Retrieval by Reformulation in Two Library Catalogs: Toward a Cognitive Model of Searching Behavior.* Ph.D. Dissertation. Madison, WI: University of Wisconsin-Madison; 1987.

9. Katzer, J.; McGill, M. J.; Tessier, J. A.; Frakes, W.; DasGupta, P. A Study of the Overlap Among Document Representations. *Information Technology: Research and Development.* 2:261-274; 1982.

10. Pao, M. L. Comparing Retrievals by Keywords and Citations. *Proceedings of the Seventh National Online Meeting*. Medford, N.J.: Learned Information; 1986: 341-346.

11. Pao, M. L.; Fu, T. T. W. Titles Retrieved from Medline and from Citation Relations. *Proceedings of the Annual Meeting of the American Society for Information Science*. 22: 120-123; 1985.

12. Pao, M. L.; Worthen, D. B. Retrieval Effectiveness by Semantic and Citation Searching. *Journal of the American Society for Information Science*. (In press).

13. Rapp, B. A. *A Comparison of Document Clusters Derived from Cocited References and Co-assigned Index Terms*, Ph.D. Dissertation. Philadelphia, PA: Drexel University; 1985.

14. McCain, K. W. Descriptor and Citation Retrieval in the Medical Behavioral Sciences Literature: Retrieval Overlaps and Novelty Distributions. *Journal of the American Society for Information Science*. (In press.)

15. Stepp, R. E.; Michalski, R. S. Conceptual Clustering of Structured Objects: A Goal Oriented Approach. *Artificial Intelligence*. 28: 43-69; 1986.

The Usefulness of Indexes: Introduction to the Theme

Our final paper is actually the first paper I commissioned for this conference. This past October [1987], I proposed the theme for this conference at an ASI board meeting held in conjunction with the ASIS conference in Boston. Dr. Ben-Ami Lipetz, a member of the ASI Board who was present at the meeting, is the author of the classic study on catalog use conducted at Yale University. I therefore asked him to do a paper on "The Use of Indexes"—what we know and which aspects need to be researched. In accepting this invitation, Prof. Lipetz asked me to modify the title to "The Usefulness of Indexes" and indicated that the paper would be based on reflections rather than research. I am sure you will find it a stimulating conclusion to the conference.

Ben-Ami Lipetz *is a professor and former dean in the School of Information Science and Policy of the State University of New York at Albany. He holds degrees in engineering and public administration from Cornell University.*

His involvement with indexes began thirty years ago, when he devised and used punched card techniques to produce and revise large printed indexes. In the sixties, he did some of the early research on automated generation of citation indexes and their evaluation. While in charge of Information Science Abstracts, *he continued to develop methods for computer-assisted generation of indexes, and he also developed and demonstrated his concept of a* continuity index, *a very compact type of index that links abstracts to each other in many ways and is amenable to automatic searching.*

Prof. Lipetz was one of the founding members of the American Society of Indexers and has served ASI at various times as a Board member and also as president.

B. H. W.

The Usefulness of Indexes

Ben-Ami Lipetz

At least some of you in this audience must have thought it rather odd when you examined the program for this conference and read through the list of papers to be presented—papers that have described and discussed all sorts of overviews and approaches and innovations and applications involving indexing—to find at the very end of that long and exciting array a final paper entitled (mystically) "The Usefulness of Indexes." I assure you that I had definite misgivings when Bella Weinberg sent me the news that I and this topic would be at the very end of the program. Surely, everyone who has already spoken today has been concerned, implicitly if not explicitly, with the usefulness of indexes. Can there be anything more to say that is worth saying, worth your listening to? You will be the judges.

Because I respect Bella and trust her skill in conference management, I accepted last place on her roster with my topic and its title that sounds very much like an introductory tutorial. I have even managed to convince myself that there is indeed some rationale for getting into this rather sweeping topic and into a rather philosophical mood at this late point in the program.

Historical studies of the sciences, I recalled, have pretty well established that in most scientific fields, perhaps all, progress comes first from current commercial, governmental, and military activity (from innovations devised for immediate limited applications), and that basic theory or broad understanding of the field tends to develop later, but often leads to further refinements of practice and to radical new applications.

The Science of Indexing

Indexing seems to fit this picture of the mainstream of science. As a practice, it goes back a long way—at least as far as the manuscript libraries of classical times, of Alexandria. Hans Wellisch has determined [1] that indexes of almost modern design and sophistication were included in some of the books published only a few decades after Gutenberg's introduction of printing technology (and before the adoption of page-numbering in books). As a skill or an art form and as a technology, indexing has grown and broadened in recent decades. The advent of information-processing machinery, especially the advent of computers, has greatly affected and stimulated the field of indexing. Yet, with all of that, as a science (as a good, reliable, predictive hard science), indexing has not yet come very far. We have lots of prescriptions, lots of hunches, about what to do in indexing, and lots of blindly accepted practices as well. Proofs of what works and what doesn't work in indexing are not totally lacking, but are quite scarce and not particularly profound. I am not by any means trying to discount the value of practical experience and good sense—but we all know that we could benefit from a more rational, better developed science of indexing than we have today. It is something we should all try to contribute to, or at least encourage.

Let me hasten to assert that, sadly, I am not about to amaze and delight you by unveiling here and now a full-blown science of indexing. I do think, however, that any emerging science advances more surely when the people engaged in that field make it a practice to back off now and then from their concentration on the details of immediate, current projects and applications, in order to reflect, constructively if possible, on the fundamental elements or concepts that define and shape the field. I would like to try that with you now. Perhaps it will turn out to be only an unneeded review of what we all know and understand fully. Perhaps it will turn out to be helpful, maybe even stimulating, for some of us.

If we want to get at the most fundamental of the fundamentals of indexing, I can see only two concepts that fall into that category: the nature of indexes, and the usefulness of indexes (what is an index?, what does it do for anyone?). I suppose that in a conference such as this there could perhaps be one or two people in the audience whose interest in indexes is only in the abstract, without regard to applications; but I am sure that most people who are concerned about indexes tend to think of indexes as tools or services, as things that are intended to be useful to other people, and that should be understood and developed in the context of usefulness. That is the sense I will try to emphasize.

Before concentrating on usefulness, let us review or summarize quickly what an index is, what it provides. To start with, an index is a list of meaningful entries, with each entry consisting of at least two components. The list or index is arranged in some logical sequence by the first component of the entries. (This is often an alphabetical arrangement of the entries, but it could just as well be some other type of logical nonalphabetic sequence, such as chronological or geographic.) The second component of an index entry is a pointer to a location of a text passage, or to a location of a record in some sort of collection, that contains or else somehow relates to the first component of the index entry. Finally, the sequence used in arranging the index is different from the sequence of the text passages or collected records to which the index points.

A function of an index, then—but not necessarily its only function—is to provide a reader or information seeker with a practical way of finding the material that is wanted within a hard-to-search text or records collection, by providing location information in an index that is presumably easier to search, for one's immediate purposes, than the text or collection itself.

This sounds quite simple. But what is it that an indexer provides, or should provide, for the reader or information seeker to look at or look up in an index? Instantly, we have all sorts of possibilities to consider. There can be indexing of names or locations or codes or dates or words or word associations or statements or concepts or concept associations, and so on. There can be heavy coverage or selective coverage in an index. There can be *see* and *see also* references to direct a reader from location to location within the index itself. The indexer does not have to stop at indexing only the terms or concepts or associations that are expressed explicitly in the text or records being indexed, but can consider indexing also by terms and concepts that come from some completely external source or authority.

An index can be made very short or very long, very simple in its design or very complex. But one thing that an index cannot be is totally exhaustive. As most of us realize and accept—sometimes only intuitively—any text or collection can be indexed to any degree or length one might imagine, and one would still, always, be able to find more entries or aspects that could logically be added to the index. Of course, one tends not to incorporate entries in an index unless they seem "useful." But deciding what to include, how much to include, how to include it, are problems in indexing that always cry out for rational, exact answers that generally elude us. Still, we know that if there are any answers to be found, they are somehow connected to the question of the usefulness, or probable usefulness, of the index that we might produce.

Subjectivity of "Usefulness"

When we try to analyze the concept of "usefulness," we get some enlightenment. But the news is mostly bad. Usefulness is not an absolute, objective quality; it is not something inherent in the thing that is useful. An index is not useful simply by virtue of its content or construction. Rather, it is useful with respect to the person who is evaluating it, and with respect to the time when the evaluation is being made, and with respect to the purpose being considered. Value (usefulness) is subjective—it is person-time-purpose related. What is exceptionally valuable to one reader may be useless to someone else, or may become useless to the first person at a later time, or vice versa. The totally accurate prediction of degree of usefulness of something like an index seems so hopelessly difficult, so complex, so impossible, that we might rather turn to witchcraft for guidance. Yet judgments regarding the probable usefulness of our indexes must be made, and are made, all the time (whether rationally or intuitively) by both the people who create indexes and the people who use indexes. It is an area worthy of much more study and research in order to put it on a dependable basis.

"Usefulness" is in the eye of the beholder. It has to do with the beholder's perception of the benefit(s) to be gained from something (such as using an index), and also with the beholder's perception of the acceptability of the costs that are paid in order to get the benefits. For the reader of an index, the benefits may be related to, say, finding a piece of information through use of the index, or to the utter relief of *not* finding something in the index, or to learning some new concept or term from the index, and, of course, to the relative values the beholder attaches to whatever benefits are found. The perceived costs may relate to purchase price or access charges, also to the time and the mental effort required to use the index, and perhaps to special equipment required, as in online searching, possibly even to the cost in storage space required to house the index. Whether the benefits are seen by the beholder as sufficient to justify the costs determines usefulness.

I realize that all of this is pretty fuzzy and perhaps even tedious stuff. So I will not elaborate further now; another time perhaps. What I am just getting around to is something a good deal more specific and, I hope, more worthwhile. I want to suggest that, even though we may not understand the notion of "usefulness" well enough to predict exactly the right index for every reader and every purpose, we can nevertheless make some fairly rational judgments about the right index products for particular populations (groups of similar people) based on observations of their actions in the past and also based on awareness of the emergence of new methods or technologies that relate to the special characteristics of some particular population.

Publishers and Book Indexing

For illustration, I would like to talk about book publishers and about how publishers treat book indexing. Many, probably most, of the people at this conference are involved in book indexing in one way or another.

Although book publishers and their editors are not the end users of book indexes, they are obviously influential in book indexing—deciding whether or not there should be any index to a book, who shall do the indexing, what length of index to require or allow, possibly deciding on some of the design and structural features of the index, and on the method of quality control to employ in checking the index. Because publishers and their staffs have the power to ordain or not ordain indexes and to shape them, it is clearly very important for indexers to understand how publishers perceive the "usefulness" of book indexes.

Now, I may be wrong, but everything I know from looking at lots of new books and from listening to the experiences of indexers leads me to believe that many, many publishers (but not all!) regard the usefulness of book indexes as small or insignificant. This does not apply to large reference books, such as encyclopedias and handbooks; but one senses it in most other types of nonfiction books that one might think deserve to have careful, extensive indexes. Many such works are published with no index at all. Many are published with only the scantiest of indexes, often poorly compiled and edited—as though an index of some type is required only for appearances, but not for consulting.

If book publishers do indeed find book indexes to be "not useful," the logic could be as follows: The objective, the desired benefit, for publishers is to make profits by selling books. If inclusion of an index, or of an extensive and careful index, will not lead to substantially greater sales, then the cost of producing and printing that index is unacceptable. And it may very well be true that, for many indexable books, the quality or even absence of an index has no important influence on sales.

Many of you are familiar with the journal called *The Indexer*. You may have noticed that one of its regular features, called "Indexes Reviewed," consists of extracts of recent book reviews that have referred to book indexes in any evaluative way. It is both surprising and discouraging to see there how often a book reviewer will criticize an index, or note the absence of an index altogether, and then go on to recommend the book most highly, or declare that a detailed table of contents makes up for the absence of an index. And these are only from the reviews that happen to make some note of indexes; usually the index is ignored completely by reviewers.

For the past ten months, I have made it my business to scan all book reviews in about forty or so American journals and periodicals, in order to add American material to the mostly British material covered by *The Indexer.* I learned that book reviewers who say anything at all about indexes are very rare, and tend to be concentrated in a few specialized journals with relatively small circulations. In the ubiquitous and highly influential *New York Times Book Review,* where I scanned reviews of many hundreds, or even thousands, of nonfiction books, only three (in ten months!) made some mention of indexing, and only very fleetingly at that. So, if the reviewers and buyers do not take book indexes very seriously (except for a few special categories of books), why should publishers? Maybe book indexes are not all that essential. Maybe readers can and do usually find what they want, fast enough and surely enough, merely by scrutinizing the contents and flipping the pages. Much as we may want to believe it isn't so, it certainly looks as though a publisher might reasonably question the usefulness of book indexes for the *publisher's* purpose of maximizing net profits from sales.

But the next point I want to make at once is that, even if such a low evaluation of the usefulness of book indexes in publishers' eyes were justified in the past, the advent of computers and databases has changed things—greatly increasing the opportunities for publishers to make new sales and increased profits through production of quality book indexes, but not from exactly the same kind of book index we have had in the past.

As we know, the book index was developed and functions to help the reader of the book. A person who is looking at a book index is already holding the book. The book and its index are printed together, bound together. The reader may well make use of the index if there is one; however, the decision to buy the book has probably either already been made without concern for the index, or—if the decision is to be made by the reader—will probably be made by looking through the text-in-hand rather than the index-in-hand.

Yet there are always large, vast numbers of people out there who have never seen, never heard of the book. Many could make use of the book. How will such people find out about the book, if ever? They are potential buyers; they can persuade librarians to buy. The books they are looking for, but unaware of, may be recent or may be quite old. But for a publisher, a sale is a sale; and such presently invisible markets could prove to be extremely large, if they can be reached.

And, in this age of computers, such markets *are* being reached by the publishers of some types of materials, through the flourishing and rapidly proliferating online bibliographic database services that searchers use heavily nowadays—that they gladly *pay* to use—in order to identify previously unfamiliar publications that will probably or possibly contain the desired material or information. And the more certain a searcher can be that an item identified this way contains what is wanted, the more likely the searcher is to get hold of a copy of the item one way or another, often by purchasing a copy.

Do indexes fit in here? Of course. An online bibliographic database is nothing more than a gigantic index that points to bare references to publications, or sometimes to references that are amplified by abstracts. In fact, many databases make an attempt to include not only journal articles and government reports and patents and so forth in their coverage, but books as well. In general, however, the coverage of books in bibliographic databases is miserably inadequate—merely indicating the main topics addressed, but not getting at the wealth of specific detail that the book may provide. Usually a database will provide more of such detail about a journal article; an article contains a smaller amount of information, and whatever information it does contain has a far greater chance of being indexed in a database than the same information if it is contained in a book. The organizations that create databases for online services are not usually geared to create detailed indexing of books. Such organizations tend to sell their products by the number of publications that are covered at all, not by the completeness of the coverage; so lengthy publications like books tend to get more cursory analysis than shorter publications.

Which brings us back to book publishers and book indexes. A publisher who is looking for evidence of the "usefulness" of book indexing should have little trouble finding it today—in online databases. Publishers should find ample incentive to contribute to the extent and the quality of coverage of their books in future databases, in order to sustain and stimulate the demand for the books that have been published. Indexers would do well to make sure that the publishers they serve are fully aware of the new opportunity.

I do not claim that this is an original or new idea. I do claim that it now deserves to be taken seriously by more people in this field. About sixteen years ago, there was an interesting pioneer effort to demonstrate that book indexes can be useful away from the books they describe. A small publishing house called R&D Press, based in the San Francisco area of California [2], issued a series of a dozen or so cumulative indexes on various scholarly topics [3]. Each of these cumulative indexes (designated "CumIndex" as a trade name) was produced by keying the indexes from a selection of the 50 or 100 books considered to be the best in that particular field and then using a special computer program to merge (smash!) all of these book indexes, with their different structures and vocabularies, into a single alphabetical sequence that proved, on the whole, to be very usable and informative; it gave easy access, precise access, and deep coverage for this selection of related books. Although still listed in the current *Books in Print*, R&D Press apparently went inactive soon after the CumIndex Series was launched, and has not continued to promote or produce this kind of publication. In retrospect, such cumulative indexes are probably economically unsuitable as print products; they are more suited to online databases. Still, R&D Press showed what is possible if book publishers were to become serious about creating and exploiting book indexing. (The many problems that R&D Press had to cope with in merging disparate book indexes also showed clearly that there is much to be gained from introducing standardized practices for book indexing.)

Increasingly, book indexers are supplying the publishers who employ them with indexes in machine-readable form, to be used in typesetting the indexes. In the future, book indexers may find themselves supplying indexes in machine-readable form also— maybe primarily, or even only—for use in online databases, to help the publisher increase sales of the books. The two different types of book indexes, print and online, would not necessarily be exactly the same, although derived from the same human analytical effort, perhaps at the same time. If they serve different purposes, there is no reason for the two types of book index to be identical in content, size, structure, or manner of presentation to users.

Summary

Perhaps I have dwelled too long on this particular excursion into what can develop from thinking carefully about usefulness. I hope that the discussion has been suggestive and stimulating.

What I have been trying to expound in this talk can be summed up in a few sentences:

—Indexing is still far from an exact science.

—The reason for having indexes, creating indexes, is to serve people who can be expected to find the indexes useful.

—Usefulness is subjective, and involves a poorly understood weighing of perceived benefits against the perceived costs of getting the benefits.

—With indexes, the perception of usefulness by readers or users is not the only important perception to consider—since publishers and other types of involved non-users (such as reviewers, librarians, jobbers, and even indexers as a group) can exert important influences on decisions regarding indexes.

—The advent of new information technologies has created new conditions that can profoundly alter the perceptions of many types of groups regarding the usefulness and feasibility of many types of indexes.

—By trying to understand the changing technological environment in terms of impacts on the benefits and costs that are important to particular groups, we can act and react more surely; that is, we can create better indexes, more useful indexes, sooner and with less risk of error.

—Even though human indexers will always remain in competition with increasingly competent computer-driven indexing, there will certainly be room for both—as long as we (the human indexers) are attentive to benefits and costs as seen by the people to be served, and as long as we are alert to the possibilities, as they arise, to create indexes that are more useful in the eyes of those to be served.

References and Notes

1. Wellisch, Hans H. The Oldest Printed Indexes. *The Indexer* 15(2): 73-82; October 1986.

2. The address of R&D Press has been given in *Books in Print* since 1972 as Los Gatos, California; on some of the R&D Press imprints, the address was given as Los Altos.

3. For example: Kilgour, Frederick G. *The Library and Information Science CumIndex*. Los Altos, CA: R&D Press; 1972. vi + 722 pp. (Information Access Series, Vol. 7). This work includes "Background of the CumIndex System" (pp. ii-v) by Series editors James L. Dolby and Howard L. Resnikoff.

Appendix

History of the American Society of Indexers

Dorothy Thomas

Founding

The idea for the American Society of Indexers was conceived at the Columbia University School of Library Service.[1] The only professional organization for indexers that existed at the time was the Society of Indexers, founded in England on March 30, 1957, as a result of the efforts of G. Norman Knight. Mary Flad, a student of Dr. Theodore C. Hines, gave impetus to the founding of the American Society of Indexers and chaired the organizational meeting on April 24, 1968. The campus on Morningside Heights was then seething with strikes and demonstrations against the Vietnam War.

A committee on organization was established at that meeting, and John Berry of the R. R. Bowker Company became chairman. In order to get a sense of what indexers wanted and needed from their organization, a questionnaire was distributed that included the very important issue of affiliation with the Society of Indexers. About ninety per cent of those answering the questionnaire favored affiliation.

Robert J. Palmer, a free-lance indexer, was going to England the following September and was asked by the committee on organization to undertake preliminary talks with the Society of Indexers. He became the corresponding member from the United States to the Society of Indexers, and was later ASI's liaison with the British.

A few months after the April meeting, Mrs. Flad moved to Syracuse, New York, and her activity in the fledgling organization ceased. Patricia Alonzo continued the development work until early fall, when she retired after the birth of her first child. Others took her place.

On November 18, 1968 the American Society of Indexers was officially founded at a meeting in New York City chaired by Dr. Theodore Hines.

Robert Palmer, having completed his mission of contacting the Society of Indexers, reported that the idea of an American Society of Indexers had been met with enthusiasm and an offer of friendship and cooperation. Dual membership (the Society of Indexers had 45 individual overseas members, of whom 31 were in the United States, and 12 institutional members, of whom 7 were in the United States), financing such membership, and support for *The Indexer* had been discussed. Since agreement on specific issues required approval of both organizations, the time had come for the formal establishment of an American Society of Indexers. The motion was made and carried, followed by a motion for the election of *pro tem* officers to serve until the next meeting, scheduled for some time around April, 1969.

Alan Greengrass, a 1968 graduate of the Columbia School of Library Service, who had become infected with Ted Hines' enthusiasm for indexing, was elected President *pro tem*, and Dr. Jessica Milstead was elected Secretary-Treasuer *pro tem*. Dues were set at $10 a calendar year, and included a subscription to *The Indexer*. A constitution committee was appointed by the President pro tem, charged with preparing a proposed document to be submitted at the next meeting of the organization. Robert Palmer was named chairman of the committee. A membership drive was initiated by way of a press release announcing the formation of the society. Published in library and book trade publications, it elicited an immediate response. By February 1969, some three months before the first annual meeting, the membership stood at 112.

The first annual meeting was held on June 16, 1969, at the Graduate Center of the City University of New York. Dr. Charles Bernier was elected President, and Eleanor Steiner-Prag was elected Vice-President (see Table 1). The constitution, of which Robert Palmer was chief architect and which was closely modeled on that of the Society of Indexers, received overwhelming approval. There was, however, an important difference between the two documents, which remains to this day. The Society of Indexers requires a potential member to pass a proficiency examination in indexing. The American Society of Indexers does not require examination, proof of expertise, or sponsorship as a prerequisite of membership.

The founders of ASI clearly knew what they were about when it came to establishing committees that the new organization would need. At the November 1969 meeting, the Program Committee; Standards, Ethics, and Specifications Committee; Membership Committee; Register Committee; and Publications Committee were established. These committees represent those areas that are still the main focus of ASI's activities. A newsletter was started early on; it was reproduced on microfiche for sale to libraries and interested people in 1987. A highly professional publication, it is now produced by desktop publishing.

Growth

The membership of the American Society of Indexers has grown slowly, albeit a bit unsteadily, showing a rise each year at the end of the school term when new library school graduates, imbued with the excitement of indexing imparted by their professors, hasten to join. Within the first year they have found employment— not always as indexers—and they often do not continue their membership. At the 1970 annual meeting, the membership was reported at 257. By the annual meeting in 1975 it had reached 266. In 1983, when ASI was fifteen years old, the number passed 500, and currently (September 1988), in the society's twentieth year, it is over 700.

As the membership has grown, so too has the need for and viability of local chapters. Though these chapters may wax and wane in membership and activity with changes in leadership, they rarely expire completely; they always seem to revive. At the present time, there are nine chapters. In alphabetical order (naturally), they are: California (Golden Gate), Chicago, Connecticut, Michigan, Minnesota (Twin Cities), New York City, Philadelphia, Utah, and Washington, D.C.

It is an unsolved curiosity that as early as the annual meeting of 1970, there was a report of a plan to form a Boston Chapter for members from New England—a logical place to have a chapter, considering the concentration of learned institutions and publishing companies in that region. Despite efforts made from then until now, that chapter has never been formed, though ASI has had a Connecticut chapter since 1987.

The members fall into three highly diverse groups, but they are interdependent in ways that are not always recognized. Some, but certainly not all of the members have had training in library and information science.

The largest percentage of members includes independent contractors—proprietors of their own indexing businesses—or freelancers, as they are often called. They produce the greatest number of back-of-the-book indexes. Increasingly, they are experts in particular disciplines, reflecting the specialization in book, serial, and periodical publishing. Some of these people are now writing book-length indexes in special fields, and it is not unreasonable to expect that they will do their own publishing in the very near future.

Corporate indexing is a new, rapidly expanding field for these indexers, as industry finds it economically justifiable to index documents from domestic and multinational operations. This is generally done on a project basis, though corporations are beginning to employ indexers in-house for this work.

This brings us to the next category of members—those who work as indexers or abstractors (or in supervisory or administrative capacities) in regular, salaried positions for business, educational, or service institutions, and for governmental agencies on all levels. Many of these people are trained librarians who specialize in indexing and abstracting for hard-copy products or online databases. Those working on databases deal in vast numbers of entries and use techniques totally different from back-of-the-book indexing, but the principles remain the same.

The third and last category of members includes those who come from academia—the teachers of indexing in schools of library and information science. These academicians produce relatively few indexes. The smallest category of ASI members, they are, however, a most important group because they are the theorists, and they annually produce new indexers. They conjecture, postulate, experiment, perform statistical analysis and advance the science and art of indexing, which in turn is put into practice by the other two categories.

Publications and Conferences

The Publications Committee has from its inception issued documents written by members, and has created and maintained publications for the Society (see Bibliography). Standards and guidelines, information on becoming an indexer, a *Register of Indexers*, a directory of indexing courses, and most recently, a book on coding for electronic markup of indexes, are among the publications. Their sale provides ASI with a continuing source of revenue, second only to dues income.

In 1978, the H. W. Wilson Company created, at the request of the Society, an award for indexing, comparable to the Wheatley Medal given by the Society of Indexers in England. The H. W. Wilson Company Award for Indexing, given for the first time in 1979, has become a much coveted prize (see Table 2). Certificates are given to the prize-winning indexer and to the publisher. In addition, the indexer receives a five-hundred dollar award.

Late in 1982, the IBM PC went on the market. The availability of reasonably priced computers produced a revolution in the profession. Indexing came out of the shoe-box and onto the floppy disk and the hard disk; the American Society of Indexers responded immediately. Members put together hardware systems, began to write indexing software, and in 1983, ASI held its first all-day meeting devoted to computer-assisted indexing, with hands-on demonstrations of hardware and software. A new column, The Electronic Shoebox, was added to the newsletter, and in 1988 a library of shareware and public domain software, available at a minimum cost to members, was established. The use of the computer for indexing has become the standard. Indexers are now designing and creating large-scale databases, and people from the database field are discovering the American Society of Indexers.

Indexing is solitary work, and the need to communicate with other indexers is satisfied by chapter and annual meetings. New York was the center of ASI for a number of years, and more annual meetings are held there than in any other city. As ASI grew, however, the annual meeting sites reflected the geographic distribution of the membership from East to West. The 1976 annual meeting was held in Chicago, the 1978 one in Washington, D.C. (the first of several meetings there), and in May 1989, the annual meeting will be held in San Francisco, when a member of the Golden Gate chapter will be installed as president.

The first meetings of ASI were limited to evening meetings; later there were all-day meetings and seminars that had overflow audiences and participants. Workshops have become highly popular events. The American Society of Indexers has begun to present programs and speakers at the conferences of the American Society for Information Science and American Library Association.

The 1988 annual meeting, held in New York, celebrated the twentieth anniversary of the American Society of Indexers. This book is a collection of the papers given at that meeting.

If one were to reckon the changes in indexing of the last twenty years, the first would be the transition from hand-written or typed indexes to computer-assisted and computer-created indexes transmitted directly to typesetters over modems or other means. The second most notable change would be the increase in the number of indexing courses given in schools of library and information science. When ASI was founded, few schools gave indexing courses. At this writing, 1988, more than 50 are given nationwide.

And if we were to reckon a constant of the last twenty years, it would be the steadfastness of the members of ASI in their devotion and dedication to the Society. Yes, there have been presidents, and secretaries, and treasurers, and they have worked diligently. But there have also been, and there still are, dozens and dozens of unnamed members across the country who plan meetings, send out notices, organize chapters, and perform the necessary functions of association management. They have enabled the American Society of Indexers to prosper and to make a continuing contribution to the publishing industry and the world of information.

Notes

1. The history of the American Society of Indexers has never been written in detail. The following articles provide some information on the early years: "Guest Editorial," *The Indexer* 6(3):90; Spring 1969; Palmer, R., "American Society of Indexers Founded in New York," *The Indexer* 6(3):91, 133; Spring 1969; "The American Society of Indexers," *The Indexer* 7(2):68-69; Autumn 1970; "The American Society of Indexers: Election of Officers and the Annual General Meeting," *The Indexer* 10(1):35; April 1976; Greengrass, A. "The American Society of Indexers (ASI)" in Knight, G. *Indexing, The Art of.* 1979: 192-193.

Bibliography: ASI Publications in Print

Education and Training in Indexing and Abstracting: A Directory of Courses and Workshops Offered in the United States and Canada, and a Bibliography of Textbooks Used in Indexing Courses. 3rd ed., by Bella Hass Weinberg. 1985.

Generic Markup of Electronic Index Manuscripts, by Hugh C. Maddocks, 1988.

A Guide to Indexing Software. Linda K. Fetters, comp. 2nd ed. 1987.

Guidelines for Publishers and Editors in Index Evaluation.

Guidelines on Employment Terms for Freelance Indexers.

Guide to Freelance Indexing, by A. Cynthia Weber, Revised 1988.

The Indexer. Semi-annual.

Indexing: A Basic Reading List, by Hans Wellisch. 1987.

Newsletter, 1-, 1970-. Five times a year.

Newsletter Index, by Shirley Thistlewood. 1985.

Newsletter and Index on Microform: issues 1-60, April 1970-Jan/Feb 1983 and *Index.*

Organizational Profile and Directory. Annual.

Proceedings of the Second Seminar on Freelance Indexing, Washington, D.C., January 13, 1979.

Register of Indexers. Annual.

So How Much Will It Cost Me? Estimating Costs and Preparing Bids for Fee-Based Information Services, by Linda Cooper. 1987.
Specifications for Computer-Based Indexes.
Specifications for Corporate-Author Indexes.
Specifications for Published Card Indexes.
Statement on Ethical Responsibility of Indexers and Index Publishers to Index Users.

Table 1

Presidents of the
American Society of Indexers

1968-69	Alan Greengrass (pro tem)
1969-70	Charles Bernier
1970-71	Eleanor Steiner-Prag
1971-72	J. Fall
1972-73	J. Fall
1973-74	Barbara Preschel
1974-75	Barbara Preschel
1975-76	Charles Bernier
1976-77	Mary Lee Tsuffis
1977-78	BevAnne Ross
1978-79	William Bartenbach
1979-80	Bernice Heller
1980-81	George Lewicky
1981-82	John Regazzi
1982-83	Mauro Pittaro
1983-84	Dorothy Thomas
1984-85	Hans Wellisch
1985-86	A. Cynthia Weber
1986-87	Ben-Ami Lipetz
1987-88	Thomas Jay Kemp
1988-89	Bella Hass Weinberg
1989-90	Nancy Mulvany (president-elect)

Table 2

Winners of the H. W. Wilson Company Award for Indexing

1988 Jeanne Moody, indexer, and National Wildlife Institute, publisher, for *Raptor Management Techniques*.

1987 Award not given.

1986 Marjorie Hyslop, indexer, and American Society for Metals, publisher, for *Metals Handbook*.

1985 Sydney W. Cohen, indexer, and Random House, publisher, for *The Experts Speak*. (Cerf and Navasky).

1984 Trish Yancey, indexer, and Information Handling Services, publisher, for *Index and Directory of U.S. Industry Standards*.

1983 Award not given.

1982 Catherine Fix, indexer, and Wm. Saunders Company, publisher, for *Diagnosis of Bone and Joint Disorders*.

1981 Delight Ansley, indexer, and Random House, publisher, for *Cosmos*. (Carl Sagan).

1980 Linda I. Solow, indexer, and M.I.T. Press, publisher, for *Beyond Orpheus: Studies in Musical Structures*.

1979 Hans H. Wellisch, author and indexer, and John Wiley, publisher, for *The Conversion of Scripts: Its Nature, History and Utilization*.

The Award is given for an index published during the previous year.

INDEX

Indexer: Bettie Jane Third